# ALLAGASH

## THE COOKBOOK

FOREWORD BY JEAN VAN ROY

INTRODUCTION BY ROB TOD

# ALLAGASH

## THE COOKBOOK

BY JAMES SIMPKINS

PHOTOGRAPHS BY BRIAN SMESTAD

Blue Tree

PORTSMOUTH

First published in the United States in 2012 by Blue Tree LLC.
P.O. Box 148
Portsmouth, NH 03802

37 10 1

*Allagash: The Cookbook* Copyright © 2012 **BLUE TREE LLC**.
Text copyright © 2012 by **JAMES SIMPKINS**.
Photographs copyright © 2012 by **BRIAN SMESTAD**.
*The foreword was translated from the French by Mike Lurquin.*

**ALLAGASH** is a federally registered trademark of Allagash Brewing Company.

First edition, October 2012

Library of Congress Cataloging-in-Publication Data available.
ISBN-13: 978-0-9802245-9-7
Printed in China.

For customer service, orders, and book projects:
Local: 603.436.0831
Toll-Free: 866.852.5357
E-mail: sales@TheBlueTree.com

www.TheBlueTree.com

Blue Tree
A BOUTIQUE PUBLISHING FIRM

## FOR SHELI

*FOR ENCOURAGING ME TO COME OUT OF HIDING,*
*AND STILL BEING HERE WHEN I FINALLY DID.*

# TABLE OF CONTENTS

ix     FOREWORD BY JEAN VAN ROY

xiii     INTRODUCTION BY ROB TOD

16     RECIPES BY REGION

19     CHAPTER 1: WHITE

33     CHAPTER 2: DUBBEL

47     CHAPTER 3: TRIPEL

61     CHAPTER 4: FOUR

75     CHAPTER 5: CURIEUX

89     CHAPTER 6: INTERLUDE

103     CHAPTER 7: BLACK

117     CHAPTER 8: VICTORIA

131     CHAPTER 9: HUGH MALONE

145     CHAPTER 10: COOLSHIP

159     ACKNOWLEDGMENTS

161     GLOSSARY

165     INDEX

# AVANT-PROPOS

Depuis plus de quarante ans, la brasserie Cantillon lutte pour sauvegarder une bière légendaire, le Lambic. Bière de fermentation spontanée de Bruxelles et de sa région, bière unique que la famille Van Roy s'évertue à promouvoir contre vents et marées.

Le combat pour la préservation de cette bière mythique s'est considérablement simplifié ces dernières années avec le retour du succès des bières de caractères et notamment des bières acides. Mais tel n'était pas le cas dans les années septante et quatre-vingt, où beaucoup voyaient le Lambic traditionnel disparaître tout simplement du monde de la bière et ce, au profit des Lambics industriels, pasteurisés et adoucis.

La cuisine à la bière a connu semblable histoire, populaire jusque dans les années cinquante et soixante, celle-ci a disparu au profit d'une cuisine plus bourgeoise souvent élaborée à base de vins lorsqu'il s'agissait de travailler un produit alcoolisé dans les ingrédients.

De part notre métier de brasseurs de Lambic, la famille Van Roy–Cantillon n'a jamais « oublié » sa cuisine à la bière, à « notre » bière. Ah les souvenirs des odeurs de carbonnades flamandes au Lambic chez ma grand-mère, les cris de joie des enfants à l'annonce de la préparation de crêpes à la Gueuze, sans oublier le classique Lapin à la Kriek et, mon favori, les boulettes à la Gueuze et aux chicons.

# FOREWORD

For over forty years Cantillon Brewery has struggled to save a legendary type of beer: Lambic. Born of spontaneous fermentation and typical of Brussels and the surrounding area, this beer is a unique product that the Van Roy family has strived to promote despite numerous obstacles and challenges.

Our efforts to keep this mythical beer alive have been considerably simplified in recent years thanks to a revived interest in full-bodied beers, in particular those with a more acidic taste. However, this was far from the case in the 1970s and 1980s, when many people expected traditional Lambic to simply disappear altogether in favor of pasteurized and sweetened industrial Lambic.

Cooking with beer also experienced a similar decline. Although popular in Belgium until the 1950s and 1960s, such dishes quickly lost ground to more upscale culinary tastes as wine became the product of choice in most recipes calling for alcohol.

Because of our profession as Lambic brewers, the Van Roy–Cantillon family never abandoned cooking with beer, in particular with our beer. I have very fond memories of the delicious smell of my grandmother's beef stew prepared with Lambic, and of seeing all the kids get excited as they learned that they were about to be treated to Gueuze pancakes. Of course there is also the classic dish of rabbit in Kriek and, my personal favorite, meatballs prepared with Gueuze and Belgian endives.

J'ai la grande chance d'avoir une maman et une épouse « cordons bleus », qui mettent autant de passion dans leur cuisine que mon père et moi en mettons dans notre brasserie. Elles n'hésitent pas à innover, à essayer des recettes nouvelles ou à revisiter des grands classiques de la cuisine belge, française ou italienne et à les adapter à la sauce « Cantillon ». Vu le peu de restaurants proposant une cuisine à la bière originale et de qualité, il nous arrive souvent d'inviter des amis étrangers à la maison afin de pouvoir leur faire déguster des plats préparés à base de Lambic, de Gueuze, ou de Kriek.

Il est dommage que nos grands chefs belges aient dénigré la cuisine à la bière ces dernières décennies au profit de saveurs plus exotiques. Nous possédons en Belgique une gamme de bières qui aurait dû inspirer nos grands chefs, qui aurait dû les pousser à promouvoir ces produits locaux, symboles de notre pays.

De nombreux chefs étrangers ont compris toute l'originalité que pouvait apporter une bière de qualité dans leurs créations. J'ai ainsi eu l'occasion de savourer de superbes réalisations à base de Cantillon en France, aux USA, ou en Scandinavie.

Heureusement, ces dernières années, de grands chefs belges ont suivi ce mouvement et ont mis tout leur savoir-faire dans l'élaboration de plats originaux. Et le succès est au rendez-vous, preuve que les amateurs étaient en demande de cuisine à la bière de qualité.

C'est donc avec beaucoup de plaisir que j'ai répondu à la proposition de mon ami Rob Tod de préfacer son nouveau livre consacré à la « food pairing » de ses très bonnes bières. Bonne lecture.

—Jean Van Roy, Cantillon Brewery

I'm very lucky to have a mother and spouse with exceptional culinary skills who are as passionate about cooking as my father and I are about our brewery. They aren't afraid to innovate, try new recipes, or take well-known Belgian, French, or Italian dishes and make them work with our Cantillon beers. In fact, I'm doubly lucky to be surrounded by these great cooks because there are so few restaurants out there offering original and good-quality beer-based dishes. As a result, we often invite friends from abroad to our home to have them taste various dishes prepared with Lambic, Gueuze, or Kriek.

I really find it a shame that Belgium's best chefs have turned their backs on cooking with beer over the past few decades to instead focus on more exotic preparations. After all, Belgium has a wide range of beers that should have served as a source of inspiration to our chefs and driven them to promote these local products, which are to a certain extent our country's trademark. Despite a lack of interest at home, however, many chefs outside Belgium understand how high-quality beer can uniquely enhance their culinary creations. As such, I have been able to taste fantastic dishes prepared with Cantillon beers in France, the United States, and the Scandinavian countries.

Thankfully, in recent years a number of top-ranked Belgian chefs have decided to take an interest in this beer renaissance and have applied their extensive know-how to developing original recipes. And wouldn't you know it, this has proved very successful, which shows that there was indeed a lot of pent-up demand for quality beer-based dishes.

So in closing, in my capacity as a great enthusiast of cooking with beer, it was with much pleasure that I agreed to write this preface to my friend Rob Tod's new book on food pairing dedicated to his excellent beers. Enjoy.

—Jean Van Roy, Cantillon Brewery

# INTRODUCTION

When Chef James Simpkins approached us two years ago with the prospect of collaborating on a cookbook, we welcomed the idea. Great food had been a part of our lives at Allagash for well over a decade, and this book seemed like a perfect natural progression.

Our relationship with food at Allagash began soon after I started the brewery in 1995, with a focus on brewing exclusively Belgian-style beers. I had always been intrigued by the almost boundless diversity among these beers, and the vast range of Belgian beer styles included the use of fruits, spices, unmalted grains, oak, wild yeasts, and bacteria cultures . . . an unlimited palate of ingredients to experiment with and create interesting favors. However, it was the very uniqueness of these beers that posed a problem: I was having a great deal of trouble selling our beers. Back then many people had never experienced the flavors in the Belgian beers, and they struggled to embrace the style.

Early on, I discovered that food pairings were a great way to introduce people to these flavors. I began to host beer dinners with restaurants and pubs that sold our beer. Pairing each course with a different beer I addressed the complementing or contrasting elements of the pairing or how the pairing enhances the overall flavor experience. A well-matched seafood entrée might bring flavors out of our Tripel that were difficult to pick up when the beer was enjoyed on its own. One of our sour spontaneously fermented Coolship beers might coax new flavors out of some Maine oysters. Food was helping people understand our beers.

Our ongoing involvement in food culture has also led us to a fulfilling relationship with the Institute of Culinary Education (ICE) in Manhattan. In fact, for the past ten years, Allagash has awarded promising ICE students scholarships for continuing education in the culinary arts.

I hope you enjoy the possibilities this book offers for the home cook and beer lover. *Allagash: The Cookbook* is more than creating great meals and pairing them with great beer—it is a journey of flavor that takes you all over America. Shop a local farm stand or bakery; visit a farmers' market or purveyor of fine cheese; savor the process of preparation. Whether by the grill or pool, urban or rural, ranch or seaside, craft your own experience as you prepare one of Chef Simpkins's recipes for yourself, family, or friends—all while enjoying Allagash beer.

We are excited about sharing this next chapter of Allagash history with you as we enter our third decade. Our mission remains unchanged since we brewed our first batch of Allagash White: to continually challenge ourselves to offer people unique experiences with beer. I am now extremely lucky to work with a team of almost fifty dedicated and passionate people who continuously push Allagash into new and exciting territory. This book offers us, and our readers, an opportunity to continue to explore and expand flavor boundaries, while experiencing two of life's greatest pleasures—great food and great beer.

—Rob Tod, Allagash Brewing Company

# RECIPES BY REGION

**NEW ENGLAND**

| | | |
|---|---|---|
| 27 | Baked Cod with Creamy Red Potatoes, Green Beans, and Heirloom Tomatoes | White |
| 41 | Herb-Roasted Leg of Lamb | Dubbel |
| 49 | Tropical Lobster Rolls | Tripel |
| 69 | Roasted Rack of Lamb with Caponata | Four |
| 77 | Maine Scallops with Caramelized Onions and Bourbon Butter | Curieux |
| 91 | Venison Tenderloin with Spiced Cranberry Relish | Interlude |
| 113 | Black Chocolate Bread Pudding | Black |
| 119 | Corn-Fried Oysters | Victoria |
| 133 | Hugh's Fish n' Chips | Hugh Malone |
| 149 | Slow-Roast Duck with Blackberry Gastrique | Coolship |

**MID-ATLANTIC**

| | | |
|---|---|---|
| 21 | Citrus Cream Crab Cakes with White Aioli | White |
| 39 | Sweet Potato Bisque with Sourdough Croutons | Dubbel |
| 55 | Soft-Shell Crab Almondine | Tripel |
| 71 | Licorice Custard with Simple Shortbread | Four |
| 85 | Vanilla Buttermilk Waffles with Apple Chutney | Curieux |
| 93 | Grilled Chicken n' Cheddar Salad | Interlude |
| 107 | Grilled Lamb Chops with White Beans and Mint Pesto | Black |
| 127 | Ginger Plum Cake | Victoria |
| 141 | Old Salt Caramels | Hugh Malone |
| 147 | Sweet and Spicy Shrimp | Coolship |

## SOUTH

| 29 | Cornbread Madeleines | White |
| 35 | Slow-Roasted Sea Salt Chicken and Collard Greens | Dubbel |
| 51 | Chicken-Plantain Roulades | Tripel |
| 67 | Chocolate Malt Bacon Water Chestnuts | Four |
| 79 | Caribbean Grilled Grouper with Spinach Salad | Curieux |
| 95 | Smoked Pork Tenderloin with Kale and Sweet Mustard Sauce | Interlude |
| 111 | Buffalo Chili with Blue Cheese Gougeres | Black |
| 121 | Open-Faced Grilled Snapper Tacos | Victoria |
| 139 | Gumbo | Hugh Malone |
| 151 | Grilled Swordfish with Peach Salsa Fresca | Coolship |

## HEARTLAND

| 23 | Chicken n' Dumplings | White |
| 43 | Chocolate Spice Cookies | Dubbel |
| 53 | Lemon-Balsamic Pear Salad | Tripel |
| 63 | Beef, Barley, Bacon Stew | Four |
| 83 | Double Cheddar Grilled Cheese Sandwich | Curieux |
| 97 | Spicy Bacon-Chili Meatloaf | Interlude |
| 105 | Cottage Pie | Black |
| 124 | Twenty-First-Century Pot Roast | Victoria |
| 137 | New York Strip Steak with IPA Cream Sauce | Hugh Malone |
| 155 | A Simple Cherry Pie | Coolship |

## WEST

| 25 | Pozole con Puerco | White |
| 37 | Stuffed Poblano Peppers | Dubbel |
| 57 | Passion Fruit Panna Cotta | Tripel |
| 65 | Gorgonzola Vegetable Tart | Four |
| 81 | Chicken Sausage Pizza | Curieux |
| 98 | Rosemary Vanilla Cream Puffs | Interlude |
| 109 | Chipotle Bacon Burger | Black |
| 123 | Ancho-Rubbed Baby Back Ribs | Victoria |
| 135 | Pad Thai | Hugh Malone |
| 153 | Chicken, Chocolate, and Chiles | Coolship |

# CHAPTER 1

# WHITE

Belgian whites, or wit beers, are unfiltered wheat beers that make use of unmalted grain in a mix of traditional malted brewing grains. The use of the unmalted grain results in more protein and gives the beer its characteristic cloudy appearance and unique flavor profile. Originally, the beer was made in the northern parts of Belgium, the Flemish-speaking area of the country, responsible for the majority of grain produced in Belgium. Spices from their northern neighbor, the Netherlands, introduced coriander and orange peel to the brewing process. Enjoyed for hundreds of years, the popularity of the beer faded with the closing of the last white beer brewery in Hoegaarden, Belgium, in the 1950s. That is until 1966, when a local milkman, Pierre Celis, created a recipe he named Hoegaarden in honor of the town. Celis went on to leave Hoegaarden and start brewing Celis White, another great representation of the style and a beer that would greatly influence the start of Allagash.

Allagash White was the first beer brewed by Rob Tod when he founded Allagash in 1995. Not content with brewing yet another lager beer, Tod was drawn to the depth and complexity of Belgian-style beers. Specifically, he had fallen in love with the Belgian white style after trying a Celis White. With limited Belgian whites with which to compare his own, Tod studied, learned, and developed his own unique version of the style. The fruit and spice character of the White are driving components. Curacao orange peel, traditional in Belgian whites, lends the beer a refreshing citrus character. Using coriander, another conventional ingredient, creates a spicy balance to the fruit. The true key to the uniqueness of Allagash White is the secret spice. Although I have been sworn to secrecy, I can tell you it gives the White a depth and finish not found in many white beers, leaving you always wanting more.

Looking back from its current success, it is with amusement that Tod recounts that people were confused about drinking a cloudy beer. "What's wrong with it?" was a typical question fielded by Tod. However, there was not much explaining necessary beyond asking people to try it. White is still the brewery's flagship beer and garners professional accolades nearly two decades after its inception.

This chapter celebrates Allagash's flagship beer. Around the table, Allagash White is easy to pair with any menu. Its full mouthfeel, uncommon in light beers, allows it to hold up against richer foods like meats or cream-based sauces, while delicate spice notes and citrus overtones serve to compliment more delicate vegetables, herbs, or seafood. One of my favorites is Chicken n' Dumplings paired with White.

Sweet crab shows off the medium body and healthy spice notes of Allagash White, while a little lemon zest mixes and mingles with the beer's balanced citrus notes. Once you try reduced cream as the binder instead of an overload of breadcrumbs, you'll never go back.

# Citrus Cream Crab Cakes with White Aioli

### WHITE AIOLI

In a mixing bowl, add the egg yolk, Allagash White, thyme, lemon zest, and salt, then whisk briefly to combine. While whisking vigorously, add the oils (together or separately) to the egg yolk mixture in a very thin stream—as the mixture thickens, you can gradually increase the pour speed. Double-check overall seasoning, then cover and set aside or place in the refrigerator.

### CRAB CAKES

In a small saucepan, bring the cream just to a boil, then simmer to reduce by half; it will thicken noticeably, get more yellow in color, and gain a sweet smell. Measure to be sure it's reduced by exactly half. When done, remove from heat, stir in the chopped thyme, and set aside to cool briefly.

In a mixing bowl, combine all remaining ingredients and mix thoroughly, then fold in the crabmeat and cream mixture, taking care not to tear apart any larger pieces and fold until uniform. Form the mixture into small cakes and sauté them over medium-high heat in grapeseed oil for 2 to 3 minutes, or until a crust forms that will let you flip them over easily. Repeat on the other side and finish in the oven for 2 to 3 minutes to warm through.

Serve with the white aioli over fresh greens or a simple salad with basil oil.

### BASIL OIL

In a blender, combine the basil leaves, oil, and small pinch of salt and blend until smooth; let stand a few hours or overnight to let flavors mature. Strain through cheesecloth if you wish. Drizzle over crab cake.

**WHITE AIOLI**
1 EGG YOLK
2 TEASPOONS ALLAGASH WHITE
½ TEASPOON FRESH THYME, CHOPPED
½ TEASPOON LEMON ZEST
PINCH OF SALT
3 TABLESPOONS GRAPESEED OIL
3 TABLESPOONS OLIVE OIL
PINCH OF GROUND CAYENNE PEPPER

**CRAB CAKES**
½ CUP HEAVY CREAM
2 TEASPOONS FRESH THYME
2 TEASPOONS FRESH BASIL, FINELY
  CHOPPED
12 OUNCES FRESH OR CANNED CRABMEAT
  (CLAW OR LUMP)
2 EGG YOLKS
2 TEASPOONS DIJON MUSTARD
½ TEASPOON CORIANDER
2 TEASPOONS LEMON ZEST
½ TEASPOON SALT
FRESHLY GROUND PEPPER, TO TASTE

**BASIL OIL**
¾ CUP GRAPESEED OIL (OR CANOLA)
½ CUP (LIGHTLY PACKED) BASIL
SMALL PINCH OF SEA SALT

I didn't like the sound of dumplings when I was younger, but then I realized they're essentially pasta! Now I love them—especially with herbs! This version features thyme because I like it so much with the White, but feel free to substitute another of your favorites! The neutral, savory flavor of the dumplings make the uniqueness of Allagash White stand out that much more—and suddenly dumplings sound really, really good.

# CHICKEN N' DUMPLINGS

### SOUP

In a soup pot, heat up the grapeseed oil and cook the onion, carrots, fennel, and sliced garlic for 2 to 3 minutes, or until slightly softened. Add chicken broth, chicken, kale, escarole, celery seed, parsley, and bay leaf; simmer for 30 minutes. Check seasoning, cover, and reduce to lowest heat.

### DUMPLINGS

In a saucepan, bring the milk, butter, salt, and thyme to a boil. Reduce heat and add the cake flour, stirring until the dough comes together. Cook for about 1 minute, stirring constantly, then remove from the stove top and place in the bowl of a mixer. With the paddle attachment on low speed, completely incorporate the eggs one at a time.

Form the dough by either rolling into "snakes" on a floured surface, then cutting into the desired sized dumpling; or by squeezing the dough from a pastry bag, simultaneously cutting to desired size using scissors or a small knife; or just drop in by the small spoonful into the simmering soup. By any method, the dumplings are cooked when they float to the surface.

Serve topped with additional fresh thyme.

### SOUP

2 TABLESPOONS GRAPESEED OIL
¼ CUP YELLOW ONION, SMALL DICE
¼ CUP CARROT, SMALL DICE
¼ CUP FENNEL BULB, SMALL DICE
1 CLOVE GARLIC, MINCED
6 CUPS CHICKEN BROTH
8 OUNCES COOKED CHICKEN
½ CUP STEAMED RUSSIAN KALE
½ CUP STEAMED ESCAROLE
½ TEASPOON CELERY SEED
1 TABLESPOON FRESH CHOPPED PARSLEY
1 BAY LEAF
SALT AND PEPPER, TO TASTE

### DUMPLINGS

1 CUP WHOLE MILK
4 OUNCES (1 STICK) BUTTER
½ TEASPOON KOSHER SALT
1 TEASPOON FRESH THYME, FINELY CHOPPED
1 CUP CAKE FLOUR
3 EGGS

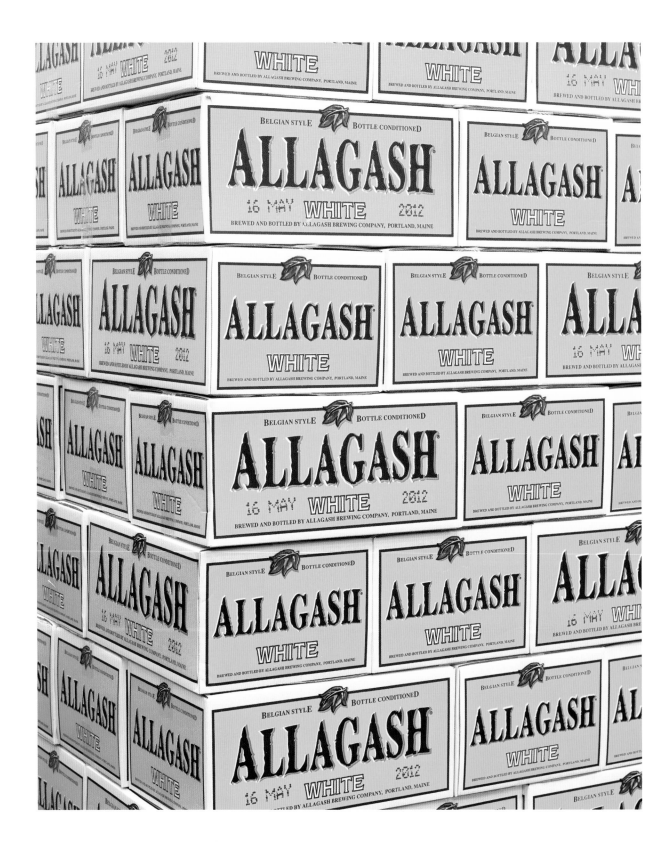

Fork-tender pork, the honest texture of hominy, and sweet-hot chiles create the background for this version of the traditional Mexican soup. Between the Aztec mythology of this southwestern staple and the inspirations behind the creation of Allagash White, this pairing really shows off the intercultural weave of American gastronomy.

## Pozole con Puerco

In a large pot, add the water and slowly simmer the pork shoulder and bay leaves for a couple of hours or until it comes apart easily with a fork (a pressure cooker is nice for this and drastically reduces cooking time). Be sure to skim the fat from the pot during or right after cooking. Once the pork is cooked, remove it from the pot and strain the cooking liquid through a fine mesh strainer, reserving this liquid. Shred the pork and put back in the pot along with the reserved cooking liquid.

Remove stems and seeds from the chiles and place in a saucepan with just enough water to cover them. Simmer the chiles until soft, then purée with some of the water they were cooked in until very smooth.

Add to the pot the garlic, cumin, and cider vinegar along with the salt, hominy, and puréed chiles and then simmer slowly for an hour. Add the oregano and thyme before checking the seasoning. Garnish with diced onion, lime juice, sliced radishes, shredded cabbage, hot sauce, or cilantro.

1½ POUNDS SHREDDED PORK SHOULDER
2½ GALLONS OF WATER (APPROXIMATELY)
2 BAY LEAVES
1 POUND HOMINY
3 TO 4 DRIED CHILES
1 WHITE ONION, DICED SMALL
4 CLOVES GARLIC, CUT IN HALF
2 SPRIGS FRESH OREGANO
1 SPRIG FRESH THYME
½ BUNCH FRESH PARSLEY LEAVES
1 TEASPOON GROUND CUMIN
1 TABLESPOON APPLE CIDER VINEGAR
SEA SALT, TO TASTE

This traditional baked cod is a simple dish but an important regional standard in Yankee cuisine. This one had to pass a few taste tests before getting the final green light! The light, smooth flavor of cod and the scent of garlic and red potatoes anchor the bright qualities of Allagash's flagship beer and make for a filling and healthy repast.

# Baked Cod with Creamy Red Potatoes, Green Beans, and Heirloom Tomatoes

## COD
Preheat oven to 350°F.

Season the cod with a bit of grapeseed oil, salt, and pepper, and place in a baking dish. In a saucepan, combine the vegetable stock, rosemary, thyme, and bay leaf and simmer for about 5 minutes. Pour the vegetable herb broth over the fish and bake in the oven until the cod flakes easily, about 25 minutes. Remove from oven and serve immediately.

## TOMATOES
Cut tomatoes in half and sprinkle with olive oil, chopped herbs, salt, and pepper. Another version is to roast the tomatoes in a slow oven (225°F) overnight, or until dried; alternately, roast in a hot oven (375°F) for about 30 minutes, or until browned and cooked through.

## POTATOES
In a saucepan, add the heavy cream, garlic, and shallots and bring to a boil; remove from heat and set aside. In another saucepan, boil the potatoes until cooked through. Strain the cooked potato halves and dry in the oven for 10 minutes. With either a potato ricer, food mill, or electric mixer, mash the potatoes into a single consistency, then add in the heavy cream and 2 ounces of the butter. Salt and pepper, to taste.

## GREEN BEANS
Steam the green beans until nearly cooked through, keeping a small crunch in the middle for texture. Drizzle with the remaining half of the butter and a touch of salt and pepper and any leftover fresh chopped herbs; toss to coat and serve immediately.

### COD
4 PORTIONS FRESH COD (24 TO 32 OUNCES)
¼ CUP GRAPESEED OIL
2 CUPS VEGETABLE STOCK OR BROTH
½ TEASPOON CHOPPED ROSEMARY
½ TEASPOON CHOPPED THYME
1 BAY LEAF
SALT AND PEPPER, TO TASTE

### TOMATOES
2 TO 3 HEIRLOOM TOMATOES, SLICED
1 TEASPOON CHOPPED PARSLEY
1 TEASPOON CHOPPED BASIL
SALT AND PEPPER, TO TASTE

### POTATOES
1 CUP HEAVY CREAM
2 CLOVES GARLIC, MINCED
2 SHALLOTS, CHOPPED
2 POUNDS RED POTATOES, PEELED AND CUT IN HALF
4 OUNCES BUTTER
SALT AND PEPPER, TO TASTE

### GREEN BEANS
1 POUND GREEN BEANS
SALT AND PEPPER, TO TASTE

One of the reasons I love madeleines (and tend to eat a lot of them) is because of how small they are—no fork required. The traditional almond and lemon flavors of these sponge cakes would be fine, but by substituting cornmeal for some of the usual flour, the madeleines pull out spice, citrus, and light cereal notes from the Allagash White—and a drizzle of honey serves as the colloquial icing.

## CORNBREAD MADELEINES

Preheat oven to 350°F.

Prepare a madeleine pan (or two) with nonstick spray and keep it at the ready.

Melt the butter in a small saucepan and set aside to cool slightly.

Whisk the flour, cornmeal, sugar, salt, and baking powder thoroughly.

In a mixing bowl, whisk the eggs, adding the melted butter in a thin stream; then add the heavy cream and whisk until incorporated.

Fold the wet and dry ingredients together until uniform, then stir in the honey.

Pour batter into the madeleine pan and bake for approximately 12 minutes, or until the edges are browned—a little longer if you want a little more color.

Let cool for a few minutes, pop out, and place on a cooling rack.

Makes about four dozen.

4 OUNCES BUTTER, MELTED
2 CUPS + 2 TABLESPOONS ALL-PURPOSE FLOUR
½ CUP + 2 TABLESPOONS FINELY GROUND CORNMEAL
A SCANT ½ CUP SUGAR
⅓ TEASPOON SALT (APPROXIMATELY)
2½ TEASPOONS BAKING POWDER
3 EGGS + 1 YOLK
2 CUPS HEAVY CREAM
2½ OUNCES EXCELLENT HONEY (WE USED SOME FROM OVERLAND APIARIES)

# WHITE

Allagash White is brewed with a blend of malted and unmalted grains, lightly hopped and spiced with Curacao orange peel, coriander, and a secret spice. Like all other Allagash beers, the White is also bottled with yeast, or bottle conditioned. Bottle conditioning not only adds to the characteristically cloudy appearance, but gives the beer a silky, full mouthfeel. The resulting beer is a delicate balance of malt, fruit, and spice that has a clean refreshing finish.

Description: Belgian-Style Wheat
ABV: 5.0%
Profile: Light, Crisp, Fruity, Spicy
Serving Temperature: 38° to 50°F
Availability: Year-Round
Package: 12oz bottle, 5.17 gallon keg, and 15.5 gallon keg
Ideal Within: Six months

# CHAPTER 2

# DUBBEL

Originally brewed by the Trappist monks of Westmalle, dubbel is one of a handful of beer styles the Belgians have chosen as their own. A dubbel is a brown ale with red hues caused by the addition of dark candi sugar. Candi sugar is a sugar syrup that provides color and also bestows flavors that lean toward burnt sugar, dried currants, and raisin. Along with the trademark fruitiness from the use of a Belgian yeast, a dubbel comes across as refined, having great balance, with hoppy undertones and a long, malty finish. The term *dubbel* (double) is likely an allusion to the perceived strength of the beer (the same is true for the tripel, or triple).

When it came to brewing a second beer, the Allagash brewers knew that they had a tall order to fill. They wanted a beer that would both stand alone and be a compliment to the White. Sticking with traditional Belgian styles, Allagash began working on its own dubbel. Their rendition is unique in a couple of ways, most notably, the use of nontraditional roasted malts. As mentioned previously, traditional dubbels achieve their color through the use of dark candi sugar. The brewers at Allagash wanted their Dubbel to be a bit more defined as a dark beer, with notes of chocolate. The resulting beer is rich, luscious, hazy dark red with a long and well-balanced finish and a complex flavor palate featuring malt, caramel, toasted nuts, and that unusual cacao-chocolate luster in the background. The hop content and 7% ABV help create a clean, dry finish that adds to the allure of the beer.

Pairing the Dubbel with food is particularly enjoyable as it lends itself to grilled meats. The candi sugar and hops allow sweeter and subtler flavors to stand out. Try the chocolate spice cookies—the creative team found them to be their hands-down favorite!

There is something to be said for anything new, especially when it actually improves on the old! Slow-roasting may be the easiest upgrade to chicken since barbecue sauce, and with Southern-style greens, it's even better. Longer, low-temp cooking times means the bird doesn't dry out and retains much more flavor and goes hand-in-hand with the full-bodied, malty, and smooth Dubbel.

# SLOW-ROASTED SEA SALT CHICKEN AND COLLARD GREENS

**CHICKEN**

Preheat oven to 200°F.

Let the chicken come up to room temperature, about 2 hours—this helps it cook evenly. Sprinkle the sea salt over the chicken. Roast in a very low-temperature oven (under 200°F) for 3 to 3½ hours, or until the internal temperature at the thigh joint reaches at least 150°F.

Let rest for 15 minutes. Cut into preferred pieces and serve over collard greens.

**COLLARD GREENS**

In a saucepan, heat up the water to nearly boiling and keep at the ready.

Chop the bacon into small pieces. In another saucepan, cook the bacon over medium-high heat. Add the butter and onions and sauté for 3 to 4 minutes, or until just softened. Add the chopped greens, sugar, vinegar, salt, and pepper. Add the heated water to the greens and bring the entire mixture to a simmer; stir until evenly combined. Let entire batch simmer for about 5 minutes, stirring every so often. Remove batch from heat before greens turn brownish.

**CHICKEN**
ONE 3- TO 4-POUND FRYER CHICKEN
GENEROUS TEASPOON SEA SALT, PLUS OR
  MINUS

**COLLARD GREENS**
4 CUPS WATER
4 OUNCES BACON
2 TABLESPOONS BUTTER
½ YELLOW ONION
4 BUNCHES COLLARD GREENS
4 TABLESPOONS SUGAR
¼ CUP APPLE CIDER VINEGAR
1 TABLESPOON SALT
1 TEASPOON FRESH BLACK PEPPER

This is a flavorful and rich recipe that pulls the nutty finish of Dubbel in a distinctly southwestern direction. And I like where it ends up—accenting the light spice of the cayenne and poblanos and the rich flavors of black beans and quinoa. Add some extra farmer's cheese to the top if you have room for it.

# STUFFED POBLANO PEPPERS

Preheat the broiler—if you have a gas stove, you can turn on a large burner for the next step instead. Place the peppers on a baking sheet (or on the burner flame) and blacken skins, turning to ensure they color evenly. When finished, place the peppers in a mixing bowl and cover with plastic wrap for about 15 minutes—this loosens the skins for easy peeling.

In a frying pan, over medium-high heat, cook the onions, mushrooms, zucchini, bell pepper, and corn for about 5 to 6 minutes, or until the onions soften. Season with salt and pepper, cumin, chili powder, and cayenne pepper and cook for an additional minute, mixing well. Remove from the heat and place the vegetable mixture in a large mixing bowl. Add the black beans and farmer's cheese to the vegetable mixture and mix well.

Place the quinoa in a saucepan and fill with water to cover the quinoa completely, then bring to a boil. As soon as the water boils, cover the pot, turn heat down to low, and simmer the quinoa for about 25 minutes until cooked through.

Preheat oven to 350°F.

Prepare a baking dish with nonstick cooking spray.

Remove the blackened poblanos from the bowl, remove skins, then clean the insides. If you want halves, cut them through; for whole peppers, just make a slit to clean the seeds from below the stem and wide enough to fill.

Fill the peppers with the black bean vegetable mixture and place them in the baking dish. Bake for 20 to 25 minutes, or until everything is heated through.

Toss the cooked quinoa with the lime juice and the remaining cilantro and top each poblano pepper. Serve right away.

4 TO 6 POBLANO PEPPERS

1 TABLESPOON CANOLA OIL
½ CUP YELLOW ONION, FINE DICE
¾ CUP MUSHROOMS, MEDIUM DICE
1 MEDIUM ZUCCHINI, MEDIUM DICE
½ RED BELL PEPPER, FINE DICE
1 CUP FRESH CORN (FROZEN IS FINE)
1 TEASPOON SALT
½ TEASPOON FRESH BLACK PEPPER
¾ TEASPOON CUMIN
¾ TEASPOON CHILI POWDER
PINCH GROUND CAYENNE PEPPER
1 POUND COOKED BLACK BEANS (ABOUT 2 CUPS UNCOOKED BEANS)
¾ CUP SOFT FARMER'S CHEESE (OR COTTAGE)

½ CUP QUINOA, RINSED
4 TABLESPOONS CILANTRO, FINE CHOP
¼ CUP LIME JUICE
SALT, TO TASTE

Sweet potatoes, along with the tang of crème fraîche and sourdough croutons, provide a full-bodied complement to the complex malt flavors in the Allagash Dubbel. The dry finish of the Dubbel helps cleanse the palate after every spoonful of soup, and the beer's nutty aromas are a natural accompaniment to the sweet potatoes. Don't stop with croutons—there's almost nothing you couldn't add to this soup.

# Sweet Potato Bisque with Sourdough Croutons

### CROUTONS
Preheat oven to 350°F.

Cut bread into larger cubes and toss in olive oil, salt and pepper, and a bit of the chopped thyme and parsley. Bake at 350°F until the croutons are crisp. Remove and cool.

### SWEET POTATO BISQUE
In a 2-quart saucepan, heat the stock, water, white wine, coriander, and bay leaf. Peel the sweet potatoes, cut into medium cubes, and place in the stock. Gently boil the potatoes until a knife goes easily in and out of them. Purée mixture in a blender until smooth, returning to medium heat and adding salt and pepper (to taste). Add half-and-half and simmer for an additional 5 minutes. Add softened butter and whisk to incorporate. Check for final seasoning and drizzle crème fraîche across the top.

Serve garnished with fresh chopped herbs and croutons.

### CROUTONS
⅓ LOAF SOURDOUGH BREAD
OLIVE OIL
SALT AND PEPPER, TO TASTE
PINCH CHOPPED THYME
PINCH CHOPPED PARSLEY

### SWEET POTATO BISQUE
ABOUT 2 POUNDS FRESH SWEET
  POTATOES (HANNAH OR GARNET)
1 QUART STOCK (CHICKEN, VEGETABLE,
  OR MUSHROOM)
2 CUPS WATER
¾ CUP WHITE WINE
1 TEASPOON GROUND CORIANDER
1 BAY LEAF
¾ CUP HALF-AND-HALF
1½ TEASPOONS KOSHER SALT
¼ TEASPOON FRESH-GROUND BLACK
  PEPPER
2 OUNCES BUTTER, SOFTENED
CRÈME FRAÎCHE

### GARNISH
1 TEASPOON CHOPPED PARSLEY
1 TEASPOON CHOPPED THYME
1 TABLESPOON CHOPPED WALNUTS

While cooking lamb usually takes a special occasion, here in the States, there's really no reason you couldn't roast a leg of lamb on some random weekend, either. Be sure to remember the Dubbel. The complex savory-sweet of the lamb and the robust malt character of this Allagash perennial have an overlap of flavor that just works, and the palate-pleasing 7% ABV ensures that one flavor group doesn't overtake the other! Don't forget to eat your vegetables.

# Herb-Roasted Leg of Lamb

**LAMB**

Preheat oven to 300°F.

Combine lemon juice, garlic, rosemary, salt, and pepper and spread over the lamb.

Roast the lamb until an internal temperature of 130° to 135°F is reached for medium rare (140° to 145°F for more medium). Approximate cooking time is 1½ to 2 hours.

Let rest 20 minutes, then slice thinly to serve.

**SIMPLE SAUCE**

Combine chicken broth and wine; reduce mixture by approximately half and add salt to taste.

Add the drippings from the roast lamb, chopped fresh herbs, and diced onion.

Check seasoning and serve.

**LAMB**

1 BONELESS LEG OF LAMB, NETTED OR TIED
3 TO 4 OUNCES FRESH LEMON JUICE
1 HEAD GARLIC, MINCED
4 TABLESPOONS CHOPPED FRESH ROSEMARY LEAVES
1 TABLESPOON SALT
2 TEASPOONS BLACK PEPPER

**SIMPLE SAUCE**

2 CUPS CHICKEN BROTH OR STOCK
1 CUP RED WINE
½ CUP CHOPPED FRESH HERBS (ROSEMARY, CHIVES, AND PARSLEY)
1 YELLOW ONION, SMALL DICE
DRIPPINGS FROM ROAST LAMB (OPTIONAL)
SALT, TO TASTE

This rich chocolate cookie is really a type of shortbread that helps pick up the nougat-y notes in the Dubbel. I think about this as a delicious, adult version of having a glass of milk with your Nestlé's Toll House. Maybe two.

# CHOCOLATE SPICE COOKIES

Preheat oven to 350°F.

Using a mixer, cream the butter and sugar (this takes several minutes), then scrape down the sides and bottom of the mixing bowl. Add the eggs one at a time, incorporating each one fully before adding the next. Scrape the sides of the mixing bowl again when finished.

In a different mixing bowl, whisk the rest of the ingredients together to form a flour-spice mix, then add to butter mixture and mix on slow speed until uniform.

Remove dough and divide in half. Roll each piece into 2- to 3-inch-thick logs, approximately the size you'd like the cookies to be. Wrap each log tightly in plastic and chill for at least 1 hour or overnight.

Line two baking sheets with parchment paper or coat with nonstick spray. Slice each log into rounds (¼ to ½ inch thick) and place 1 inch apart on prepared baking sheets. Bake cookies until slightly crisp, 8 to 10 minutes, then let cool completely. Repeat with any remainder of the dough.

6 OUNCES UNSALTED BUTTER AT ROOM
   TEMPERATURE
1¾ CUPS SUGAR
2 EGGS, BEATEN

3 CUPS ALL-PURPOSE FLOUR
1 CUP EXCELLENT
   (UNSWEETENED) COCOA POWDER
1 TEASPOON CINNAMON
1 TEASPOON DRIED GINGER
½ TEASPOON FRESHLY GROUND BLACK
   PEPPER
¼ TEASPOON SALT
PINCH CAYENNE PEPPER

# DUBBEL

Allagash Dubbel is brewed with a blend of eight different malts, including a not-quite-traditional roasted malt. Like most of our beers, the Dubbel is hopped just enough to maintain a balance between bitter and sweet. We also add a portion of dark candi syrup to the brew that serves to both add fermentable sugars and a raisin-like flavor. Allagash Dubbel boasts a deep red color and a complex malty taste. The finish is dry with subtle hints of chocolate and nuts. Our house yeast asserts itself by lending a classic Belgian fruitiness.

Description: Belgian-Style Dubbel
ABV: 7%
Profile: Deep Red, Dry, Nutty
Serving Temperature: 40° to 50°F
Availability: Year-Round
Package: 12oz bottle, 750ml bottle, and 5.17 gallon keg
Ideal Within: One Year

# CHAPTER 3

# TRIPEL

As with the dubbel style, the Belgian tripel is an old term of reference but standardized as an official style much more recently. Originally referred to as *superbier* by the monastic brothers, tripels are brewed using a high concentration of pilsner malt helping to develop the trademark golden amber color, as well as a polished mouthfeel and subtropical sweetness. These attributes plus a refreshing, refined character make it easy to drink. A rather strong beer (8–10% ABV) it is one of the most popular beer styles in Belgium.

Tripel was added to the brewery's repertoire to help firmly establish Allagash as a brewery based on Belgian tradition and technique. Allagash Tripel is probably its most traditional attempt at brewing a classic Belgian style. The grain bill and hop profile are fairly simple and within style guidelines. The true uniqueness of this beer lies in the use of the Allagash house yeast. The simplicity of the Tripel allows the spice and passion fruit character of the yeast to take center stage. Allagash Tripel is one of its most celebrated beers in the tripel style, earning mentions in reference texts and articles, not to mention a few awards along the way.

At the table the strengths of the Allagash Tripel are light, but its intense and complex flavors that enhance crab and strong cheeses such as Stilton. The use of the beer's passion fruit, herbal notes and suggestions of banana and honey blends harmoniously with fruity desserts or cookies. The tropical lobster roll is a must-try with the lemon-balsamic salad and a panna cotta for dessert?

Because Allagash headquarters is in the heart of lobster country and the locals love this New England dish, the lobster roll practically demanded a place in this book. The dilemma was that everyone already makes them—but not with mango. Lobster, mango, and the passion fruit notes that permeate the long, mouth-watering finish of Allagash Tripel make the case that even classics can have room for improvement.

# TROPICAL LOBSTER ROLLS

**AIOLI DRESSING**

In a bowl, whisk together the egg yolk, lemon juice, salt, and cayenne pepper, then drizzle in the oils (together or separate) until incorporated and the mixture has thickened. Stir in chopped tarragon, scallions, lemon zest, and orange zest and check seasoning.

**LOBSTER ROLLS**

Dice the lobster meat into small chunks and place in a bowl. Add the chopped celery stalks, mango, and 75 percent of the aioli dressing, then check seasoning, adding more of the dressing if you wish; set aside.

Toast the dinner rolls until a light crust forms, then lightly butter the insides. Divide lobster mixture among the rolls, drizzle a bit of melted butter on each, and top with additional sliced scallions, chopped tarragon, celery leaves, and/or diced mango.

**AIOLI DRESSING**
1 EGG YOLK
3 TEASPOONS LEMON JUICE, FRESHLY SQUEEZED
½ TEASPOON SALT
PINCH OF CAYENNE PEPPER
½ CUP GRAPESEED OIL
¼ CUP EXTRA-VIRGIN OLIVE OIL
½ TEASPOON FRESH TARRAGON, FINELY CHOPPED
1 TEASPOON SCALLION, FINELY SLICED
1 TEASPOON LEMON ZEST
¼ TEASPOON ORANGE ZEST

**LOBSTER ROLLS**
1 POUND COOKED LOBSTER MEAT
2 INNER STALKS CELERY (WITH LEAVES), FINELY DICED
4 DINNER ROLLS
2 TABLESPOONS UNSALTED BUTTER, MELTED
2 GREEN ONIONS (SCALLION), FINELY SLICED
½ MANGO, FINELY DICED
SALT AND FRESHLY GROUND PEPPER, TO TASTE

The Tripel's hop-induced bitterness and tropical fruit aromas contribute mightily to the allure of this Caribbean-influenced dish. The savory yet mild flavor of chicken and plantains is enhanced with the addition of prosciutto. Shaved coconut gives a tinge of sweet, and cilantro-mint sauce provides pizazz.

# CHICKEN-PLANTAIN ROULADES

### CHICKEN ROULADES
Preheat oven to 350°F.

Pound chicken breasts flat under plastic wrap, then season with a bit of grapeseed oil and fresh pepper. Place 1 to 2 slices of prosciutto on top of each breast.

Peel and cut the plantain into quarters. Place one on each chicken breast, season with a bit of grapeseed oil, and roll up each breast—using a toothpick or two to keep them together. Coat each breast in flour, then egg, then grated coconut.

Arrange chicken in a baking dish prepared with nonstick spray and cook for approximately 25 to 30 minutes, or until fully cooked. Let cool for 5 to 10 minutes, slice on a diagonal, and serve with cilantro-mint purée.

### CILANTRO-MINT SAUCE
In a food processor, combine parsley, cilantro, mint, pine nuts, vinegar, lemon/lime juice, coriander, salt, white pepper, and hot sauce; pulse the blades to process until ingredients form a paste. Leaving the processor running, pour the oil in a thin stream through the feed tube. Transfer to a bowl and chill for 20 minutes. Serve with the chicken roulades.

### CHEF'S NOTE
This recipe makes a substantial appetizer, or add a side dish of roasted vegetables or sweet potatoes and it's dinner. And the sauce is also a great accompaniment with fish and salads.

**CHICKEN ROULADES**
4 CHICKEN BREASTS
GRAPESEED OIL
FRESHLY GROUND PEPPER
4 TO 8 PROSCIUTTO SLICES
1 RIPE PLANTAIN
1 TO 2 TABLESPOONS FLOUR
1 EGG + 2 TABLESPOONS WATER, BEATEN
1 CUP GRATED COCONUT

**CILANTRO-MINT SAUCE**
¼ CUP PARSLEY LEAVES *
1 CUP CILANTRO LEAVES *
¼ CUP MINT LEAVES *
¼ CUP PINE NUTS
2 TABLESPOONS RICE WINE VINEGAR
2 TABLESPOONS LEMON/LIME JUICE
½ TEASPOON CORIANDER
1 TEASPOON SALT
⅛ TEASPOON WHITE PEPPER
HOT SAUCE, A FEW DASHES
¼ CUP GRAPESEED OIL

* LOOSELY PACKED

In this salad the lemon juice lightens up the balsamic vinegar and blends with the pear to highlight the classic fruitiness of Belgian yeast in the Tripel. The savory, salty Stilton and walnuts provide earthly and heavenly complements. Because of the rich flavors of all of the salad's components, one could argue that, with a glass or two of Tripel, it may make for a meal.

# Lemon-Balsamic Pear Salad

**DRESSING**

In a mixing bowl (or food processor or blender) combine vinegar, lemon, honey, parsley, zest, and salt; mix or pulse briefly to combine. While whisking (or with the blades spinning), begin to add the oil—at first a drop or two at a time, then in a very thin stream until the dressing is emulsified. Check seasoning and set dressing aside.

**PEAR SALAD**

Core and slice the pear very thinly and set aside. In a mixing bowl, add the frisée, arugula, and dressing (to taste); mix to combine. Place salad in a serving bowl or on individual plates and garnish with the cheese, cranberries, walnuts, and sliced pear. Serve immediately.

**DRESSING**

2 TABLESPOONS BALSAMIC VINEGAR
2 TABLESPOONS FRESH LEMON JUICE
1 TABLESPOON HONEY
1 TABLESPOON CHOPPED PARSLEY
1 TEASPOON LEMON ZEST
1 TEASPOON KOSHER SALT
¼ CUP GRAPESEED OIL

**PEAR SALAD**

1 TO 2 HEADS (DEPENDING ON SIZE), FRISÉE LETTUCE, CHOPPED
3 OUNCES (APPROXIMATELY) ARUGULA
3 OUNCES STILTON CHEESE, CRUMBLED
¼ CUP DRIED CRANBERRIES
½ CUP WALNUT HALVES, LIGHTLY TOASTED AND CHOPPED
1 PERFECTLY RIPE PEAR (COMICE OR ANJOU)

Being from Ohio, my first experience with soft-shell crabs naturally did not happen there, but culinary school and living in New York changed that. It only took one soft-shell sandwich and I was in love. Crab and almond with pungent parsley makes for a great lunch. Add a strong aioli and a glass of Tripel and it's a memory you'll hang on to for a while.

# Soft-Shell Crab Almondine

In a mixing bowl, add both flours, salt, and pepper, and whisk to combine. In a separate small bowl, whisk the egg whites until just frothy. Coat each crab in the egg whites, then dredge them in the flour mixture—shake off any excess and set aside.

Heat half the olive oil in a large skillet over medium-high heat. Place the crabs, belly side down, and cook until browned and crisp. Remove crabs to a plate, add remaining olive oil, then return to the pan to brown the other sides for an additional few minutes. Return crabs to the plate and let drain.

Drain any excess oil from the skillet, then return to high heat and deglaze the pan with the white wine, letting it cook down a little. Add the butter and almonds and cook for 1 minute over high heat. Turn off the heat, add parsley, and stir to combine.

⅓ CUP FLOUR
⅓ CUP ALMOND FLOUR
½ TEASPOON SALT
PINCH OF FRESHLY GROUND BLACK
   PEPPER
2 EGG WHITES, BEATEN
4 SOFT-SHELL CRABS
3 TABLESPOONS OLIVE OIL
¼ CUP WHITE WINE
2 OUNCES BUTTER
¼ CUP SLICED ALMONDS
1 TABLESPOON PARSLEY, FINELY CHOPPED
LEMON WEDGES
3 TO 4 OUNCES OF BIBB LETTUCE

Serve crabs over the greens, drizzling each with some of the almond-parsley mixture and a lemon wedge.

**CHEF'S NOTE**
You can serve this with the white aioli (*see page 21*), and feel free to substitute Allagash White in the recipe with the Tripel.

Panna cotta is an easy-to-prepare dessert, especially delicious with vanilla bean and passion fruit, and it goes perfectly with Allagash Tripel. For a beer with a high ABV (9%), the Tripel remains smooth and balanced and doesn't intrude on the panna cotta—and the honey and herbal notes show up with gusto. A great take on dessert!

## Passion Fruit Panna Cotta

Combine half-and-half, cream, vanilla bean, sugar, and gelatin and heat until the gelatin dissolves—do not boil. Strain the milk mixture into a mixing bowl and stir in the passion fruit juice. Pour cream mixture into molds; cover and refrigerate until they are set. Peel and cut mango into thin slices. Invert panna cotta onto serving dish and garnish with sliced mango and extra passion fruit juice.

1 CUP HALF-AND-HALF
1 CUP WHIPPING CREAM
½ VANILLA BEAN, SPLIT AND SCRAPED
¼ CUP SUPERFINE SUGAR
2 TEASPOONS POWDERED GELATIN
⅓ CUP PASSION FRUIT JUICE (STRAINED)
1 WHOLE MANGO AND EXTRA PASSION
    FRUIT FOR GARNISH

# TRIPEL

Allagash Tripel is brewed with a surprisingly simple grain bill consisting of just two malts. Though lightly hopped, the clean character of this beer allows the hops to gently express themselves. The addition of light candi sugar helps to boost the alcohol level and give the beer a clean, dry finish. Fermented with our house yeast, this strong golden ale is marked by passion fruit and herbal notes in the aroma, with suggestions of banana and honey in the complex palate. At 9% ABV, the Tripel is remarkably smooth and easy to drink.

Description: Strong Golden Ale
ABV: 9%
Profile: Honey, Passionfruit, Herbal
Serving Temperature: 40° to 50°F
Availability: Year-Round
Package: 12oz bottle, 750ml bottle, and 5.17 gallon keg
Ideal Within: One Year

# FOUR | ALE

Allagash takes great care in staying connected to its traditional Belgian roots yet has established a practice of challenging the boundaries of what makes a beer Belgian, or traditional. Allagash Four is a noble example of how pushing all the limits at once can be a good thing.

Allagash's Four is basically a double dubbel, which would make it a quad in the newly defined Belgian brewing style. The brewers at Allagash had been thinking about creating a quad for a while, and by chance the calendar helped make that decision—releasing Allagash Four on 4/4/04. Rob had the idea to brew the beer with four malts, four sugars, and four hop varieties, and then ferment it four times using four different yeast strains. The complexity of the brewing process creates this unique beer with a lush mahogany color, intense malty nose, and flavors of raisin, strawberry, candied fruit, and plum. Boasting an ABV of 10%, there are at least a few echoes of barley wine, but the brew stays balanced throughout its seemingly endless finish and invites consideration and reconsideration of its flavors. Even after drinking it several times, there may be room to find something new in the experience.

In the kitchen, consider matching Four with sweet-savory foodstuffs like bacon or chocolate for an avalanche of flavor, while even-keeled grain salads create a yin-yang-like contrast. Meats and strong cheeses also pair well. In this chapter, don't miss the gorgonzola vegetable tart and the bacon-wrapped chocolate-malted water chestnuts—both are exceptional accompaniments to this special beer.

Stewing meats is one of the oldest, simplest methods of cooking and allows for a great variety of flavors, though this one is intended to have a few more flavors in it than the stews I grew up eating. This stew came about after referring to Allagash Four as sturdy in one of my tasting notes, then making an effort to capture the multi-layered grain, malt, fruit, and yeast notes with what I came up with. I don't know if sturdy is a technical term, but I like how it came out.

## BEEF, BARLEY, BACON STEW

Place the bacon in a soup pot and cook until well-browned. Remove the bacon to drain on a paper towel, leaving the rendered fat in the pot. Dredge the beef in the flour, salt, and pepper. Knock off excess and sear the beef in the bacon fat.

Remove beef from the pot, increase heat to high, and cook the garlic and half the portion of onion, fennel, and parsnip for approximately 3 minutes. Deglaze with Allagash Four and stir well. Add the beef stock and bring to a simmer, then strain the entire mixture through a sieve or a fine mesh strainer. Reduce the heat to low and add the barley and let simmer for about 45 minutes, stirring at intervals.

After 20 minutes, add the potato and remaining batch of onion, fennel, and parsnips and let simmer for another 15 to 20 minutes, or until the vegetables are al dente.

Add the butter, then check the seasoning. Garnish with the cooked bacon and a drizzle of crème fraîche before serving.

8 OUNCES BACON, MEDIUM CHOP
1½ POUNDS STEW BEEF, LARGE CHUNKS
½ CUP FLOUR
½ TEASPOON KOSHER SALT
FRESHLY GROUND PEPPER, TO TASTE

1½ RED ONIONS, MEDIUM DICE
4 CLOVES GARLIC, MINCED
1½ FENNEL BULBS, MEDIUM DICE
1½ LARGE PARSNIPS, MEDIUM DICE
1½ CUPS ALLAGASH FOUR
3 TABLESPOONS BUTTER
4 CUPS BEEF BROTH
1 RUSSET POTATO, MEDIUM DICE
½ CUP BARLEY
SALT AND PEPPER, TO TASTE

2 OUNCES CRÈME FRAÎCHE

Given its strong scent, Gorgonzola cheese is particularly suited for blending; I find only true fans eat it solo. For the rest of you, it's also great with edibles like squash, spinach, or with a buttery tart shell, and its rich texture and unique character make it impossible to replicate—just like Allagash Four. The tart is almost sweet, but savory and pungent. It blends with all the moving components of the Four, with each one ever so slightly improved by the other.

# Gorgonzola Vegetable Tart

**TART DOUGH**

Put the flour and salt in a mixing bowl and fit a countertop mixer with the paddle attachment. Place the butter in with the flour and turn the mixer on the lowest speed. Keep an eye as the mixer works the butter into the flour, turning off the mixer occasionally to check the size of the remaining butter. Stop mixing when any remaining bits are about the size of peas. Strain any ice cubes from the water and turn the mixer back on low speed. Carefully add the ice water, a tablespoon at a time, letting each addition mix in for a few seconds before adding more. The dough is done when a small addition of water begins to peel the dough back cleanly from the edges of the mixing bowl.

Divide dough into two balls, flatten them into discs, and refrigerate for about an hour. Roll out one of the disks to approximately one-eighth-inch thickness. Form the dough inside a tart pan (hopefully one with a removable bottom) and chill in the refrigerator for 30 minutes.

**FILLING**

Preheat oven to 400°F.

**TART DOUGH**
12 OUNCES ALL-PURPOSE FLOUR
½ TEASPOON SALT
8 OUNCES BUTTER (2 STICKS), COLD AND
   CUT INTO SMALL CUBES
½ CUP ICE WATER, PLUS OR MINUS

**FILLING**
1½ CUPS HEAVY CREAM
2 LARGE EGGS + 2 YOLKS
¼ CUP FRESHLY GRATED PARMESAN
   CHEESE
¼ TEASPOON FRESHLY GRATED NUTMEG
12 OUNCES BABY SPINACH
½ TEASPOON SALT
1 POUND BUTTERNUT SQUASH
2 TABLESPOONS OLIVE OIL
FRESHLY GROUND BLACK PEPPER
5 OUNCES GORGONZOLA CHEESE,
   CRUMBLED OR CUT INTO SMALL PIECES

Prick the bottom of the tart shell all over with a fork and line it with parchment paper. Fill with dried beans or heat-proof weights, and bake for 15 minutes (this keeps the shape of the crust while it bakes). Remove the parchment paper and weights and bake a few more minutes, until the crust is a light brown. Transfer the baked tart shell to a cooling rack.

Peel and thinly slice the squash, then toss with 1 tablespoon olive oil, salt, and pepper, and place on a walled baking sheet for 15 to 20 minutes, or until the squash is tender. Cook the spinach in 2 tablespoons olive oil in a covered saucepan for about 30 seconds, just to wilt it, then drain and set aside. Whisk the eggs, yolks, cream, Parmesan, nutmeg, and salt and pepper together. Gently wring the water from the spinach and spread it evenly about the pastry shell. Follow with a layer of Gorgonzola and squash, then pour the egg mixture evenly over the top. Bake for about 30 minutes, or until the middle just sets. Let cool before serving.

These bite-sized creations are designed to provide a multilevel taste experience like Allagash Four, whose flavor components are developed through a highly complex brewing and fermentation process. The complexity (and a certain amount of delight) in this dish is brought about by the richness of chocolate, the unmistakable tang of malt, and bacon. For best results, make two times the recipe—they go fast.

## CHOCOLATE MALT BACON WATER CHESTNUTS

Preheat oven to 350°F.

Cut each strip of bacon in half and wrap the water chestnuts with them. Secure with a wooden toothpick and place in a baking dish.

Bake for about 10 minutes.

In a saucepan, combine water and sugar to make a simple syrup. Place in the top of a double boiler with the chocolate and chocolate malt powder, heat, and stir until smooth.

Cover each chestnut with the chocolate malt mixture and bake for 5 to 10 additional minutes, or until bacon is crispy.

For a more balanced bite, bake the chestnuts fully and then drizzle with the chocolate sauce.

1 POUND CENTER-CUT BACON
2 CANS OF WATER CHESTNUTS (8 OUNCES EACH)
¼ CUP WATER
2 OUNCES SUGAR
2 OUNCES CHOCOLATE, DARK
1 TO 2 TEASPOONS CHOCOLATE MALT POWDER

There are many intriguing layers of flavor in the Allagash Four ale, and this recipe deliberately meets them all head-on. Caponata is an ingredient and time-heavy dish to prepare, but not especially complicated in contrast to its rich, chutney-like sweets and sours. These, along with the multifaceted flavors of lamb and golden raisins, echo the malty, sweet, dried fruit notes in the Four. This combination is a good one to share, particularly with foodies.

## ROASTED RACK OF LAMB WITH CAPONATA

Preheat oven to 400°F.

### LAMB

In an ovenproof pan, sear the lamb on each side for about 2 minutes until well-browned. Season with salt and pepper and place the skillet in the oven and cook until the desired internal temperature is reached—approximately 15 minutes for medium.

### CAPONATA

In a large sauté pan, add the eggplant and cook until browned and drain on a paper towel.

Add the onion and fennel and sweat over medium heat for 4 to 5 minutes, or just softened. Add the tomato purée, some of the water, and a pinch of salt and simmer for 6 to 8 minutes.

Return the eggplant to the pan and add the olives, capers, vinegar, raisins, celery, pine nuts, parsley, and oregano. With a mortar and pestle, pound the rosemary leaves combined with olive oil and salt and pepper—add to the sauté pan at the end and stir in.

Turn off heat, cover, and let sit for 15 minutes before serving.

**LAMB**
2 TABLESPOONS OLIVE OIL
FOUR HALF-RACKS OF LAMB (BONES SCRAPED CLEAN)

**CAPONATA**
¼ CUP GRAPESEED OIL
2 MEDIUM EGGPLANTS, MEDIUM DICE + 2 TEASPOONS SALT (TO RELEASE WATER)
1 RED ONION, MEDIUM DICE
1 LARGE FENNEL BULB, MEDIUM DICE
PINCH KOSHER SALT
1 CUP TOMATO PURÉE
½ CUP CASTELVATRANO OLIVES, PITTED AND CHOPPED
2 TABLESPOONS BABY CAPERS
¼ CUP RED WINE VINEGAR
¼ CUP WHITE WINE
½ CUP GOLDEN RAISINS
½ CUP CELERY, SMALL DICE
½ CUP RAW PINE NUTS
¼ CUP ITALIAN PARSLEY
1 TEASPOON FRESH OREGANO, FINELY CHOPPED

2 TEASPOONS FRESH ROSEMARY, FINELY CHOPPED
2 TABLESPOONS EXCELLENT OLIVE OIL
SALT AND FRESHLY GROUND PEPPER, TO TASTE

88

84

81

77

74

70

67

63

60

65

30

The custard itself is a refreshing dish you can serve alone or with additions like fresh berries. With a few shortbread cookies and a glass of Allagash Four, you might confuse your kitchen with a patisserie. The heady licorice notes and mildly sweet shortbread follow the lead of the Four—and all happily arrive together.

# LICORICE CUSTARD WITH SIMPLE SHORTBREAD

**LICORICE CUSTARD**

**LICORICE CUSTARD**
1 OUNCE CORNSTARCH
1 QUART + ½ CUP MILK
¼ CUP EXCELLENT SOFT BLACK LICORICE, MINCED
⅛ TEASPOON SALT
⅓ CUP + 2½ TABLESPOONS SUGAR
3 EGG YOLKS
1 OUNCE BUTTER, ROOM TEMPERATURE

In a mixing bowl, combine the cornstarch and ½ cup milk.

In a saucepan, over medium heat, combine the licorice, salt, quart of milk, and ⅓ cup of sugar, whisking briskly to help licorice dissolve. Cook until the licorice dissolves, approximately 20 minutes. While whisking, pour the cornstarch mixture into the milk mixture and cook for 1 to 2 minutes until fully thickened.

In a medium bowl, whisk together egg yolks and the 2½ tablespoons of sugar until combined. Add the hot milk mixture in a slow stream. Return this mixture to the saucepan, add butter and cook over moderate heat, stirring constantly until the mixture thickens (just over 160°F).

Pour the mixture through a fine-mesh sieve into a storage bowl. Store with a layer of plastic wrap covering the custard and another sealing the container. Let set overnight, or at least four hours.

**SIMPLE SHORTBREAD**

**SIMPLE SHORTBREAD**
2 CUPS FLOUR
¼ TEASPOON SALT
8 OUNCES BUTTER (2 STICKS), ROOM TEMPERATURE
1 TEASPOON PURE VANILLA EXTRACT
½ CUP CONFECTIONERS' SUGAR

Preheat oven to 350°F.

In a mixing bowl, add the flour and salt and whisk to combine. In the bowl of a mixer, cream the butter, vanilla, and sugar together (approximately 3 minutes), scraping the sides of the bowl after it's finished. With the mixer on the lowest speed, add the flour mixture all at once and mix until the dough is just combined.

Roll dough into two cylinders in the desired width of the cookie. Chill in the refrigerator for at least 30 minutes, then slice into cookies approximately ½ inch thick.

Bake for approximately 15 minutes or until the edges have slightly darkened.

OUR | ALE

S 4HOPS *fermented* 4TIME

AGAS

# FOUR | ALE

Allagash Four is brewed with four malts, four sugars, and four hop varieties, and we ferment it four times, using four different yeast strains. The complexity of the brewing process is matched only by the complexity of this unique beer. Flavors of raisin, candied fruit, and plum express themselves throughout. The strong malt backbone gives way to a surprisingly dry finish. The four different yeast strains express themselves at different points in the drinking of this intricate beer.

Description: Belgian-Style Quadruple
ABV: 10%
Profile: Mahogany, Complex, Candied, Malty
Serving Temperature: 40° to 50°F
Availability: Year-Round
Package: 750ml bottle, 5.17 gallon keg
Ideal Within: Two Years

# CHAPTER 5

# CURIEUX

Curieux was Allagash's first foray into barrel aging beers . . . a happy accident. It seems that a batch of Tripel was waiting to be packaged for sale, but there was a hold-up on a delivery of bottles being shipped from Belgium. Coincidently, the brewery had just received a shipment of used bourbon barrels from Jim Beam for aging the Allagash Dubbel. At the time, not too many breweries were barrel aging beer and conventional wisdom was to do it with darker varieties. However, necessity pulled the brewers in a different direction. Since bottling Tripel wasn't an option, the team voted to age the Tripel in a few of the barrels, thinking that aging a light-colored beer could be interesting. The gamble paid off; within a month it was clear that it was going to be a success, and it continues to be one of the more sought-after beers Allagash offers.

What makes this particular beer curious is that there are meta-flavor layers; meaning the beer is simultaneously two versions of itself. A batch of Tripel is aged in Jim Beam bourbon barrels for six to eight weeks in the Allagash cold cellars, then the aged beer is blended back with a portion of a fresh batch of Tripel. The resulting beer has a soft mouthfeel like its original form featuring notes of coconut, tropical fruit, and vanilla; however, the Curieux also has increased complexity, hints of bourbon, and an aggrandized ABV of 11%.

For a high-gravity beer, the Curieux is surprisingly nimble around a variety of foods. More predictable pairings include smoked meats and barbecue—especially with plenty of sauce—as well as strong cheeses like Roquefort, Gorgonzola, or Stilton. Curieux has a way of yielding to other flavors, such as tropical fruit and seafood. Standouts in this chapter include Maine scallops with bourbon butter, the vanilla waffle with apple chutney, and the double cheddar grilled cheese.

This recipe recreates a dish I made for a dinner at Rob Tod's house—a dinner that eventually turned into this book. Everyone at the table that night thought this was the standout, especially given how relatively simple it is to prepare. The mellow brine of the scallop makes Curieux's complexity even more so, while the sweet and sour of bourbon echo in both the butter sauce and the beer. Better bourbon makes it . . . better.

# MAINE SCALLOPS WITH CARAMELIZED ONIONS AND BOURBON BUTTER

Preheat oven to 350°F.

Clean scallops and pat them dry with a paper towel. Lightly season with freshly ground pepper and set aside.

In a large sauté pan, heat the grapeseed oil until the first wisps of smoke appear. Sear the scallops until well-browned on one side. Flip and immediately put in the oven and bake for 4 to 5 minutes and set aside.

Serve with the caramelized onions, bourbon butter, and drops of parsley oil.

## BOURBON BUTTER
In a mixing bowl, whisk the butter, bourbon, and salt and pepper until uniform. Check seasoning.

## CARAMELIZED ONIONS
In a skillet, over medium-high heat, add the canola oil and sauté the onions until they soften and turn translucent, stirring occasionally. Add the salt, and lower the heat to medium. Cook until the onions on the bottom begin to brown, stirring only when necessary to keep them from burning. Continue in this manner until the onions are a rich brown color—or they are to your liking.

Add the butter, stir to incorporate, and then remove the onions from the pan and spread in a thin layer on a flat surface to cool.

## PARSLEY OIL
Place the canola oil and parsley leaves in a blender and purée until smooth. Use as is, or strain if you wish.

### SCALLOPS
12 LARGE SCALLOPS
¼ CUP GRAPESEED OIL

### BOURBON BUTTER
6 OUNCES BUTTER, ROOM TEMPERATURE
1½ OUNCES EXCELLENT BOURBON
SLIGHTLY COARSE SEA SALT
FRESHLY GROUND BLACK PEPPER

### CARAMELIZED ONIONS
2 YELLOW ONIONS, MEDIUM SLICED
2 TABLESPOONS CANOLA OIL
PINCH OF SALT
PAT OF BUTTER

### PARSLEY OIL
¾ CUP CANOLA OIL
¾ CUP LOOSELY PACKED PARSLEY LEAVES, STEM FREE

Though Curieux is known for its bourbon barrel aging process, this recipe takes aim at the beer's coconut and vanilla tones and puts them with tropical fruit, spinach, and a little heat. Another mild, firm-fleshed whitefish can be substituted for grouper, but nothing can substitute for the Curieux.

# CARIBBEAN GRILLED GROUPER WITH SPINACH SALAD

Preheat grill.

**CARIBBEAN BBQ SAUCE**
In a saucepan, combine the first nine ingredients (mango juice, apricot preserves, lime zest, lime juice, honey, ginger, ground cumin, ground cinnamon, and jalapeño pepper) and a pinch of salt and barely; bring to a boil. Stirring frequently, reduce the heat and simmer for about 15 minutes, or until noticeably thickened. Remove from the heat and set aside.

**SPINACH SALAD**
In a mixing bowl, whisk vinegar, honey, paprika, poppy seeds, and salt. While whisking the vinegar mixture, add the grapeseed oil in a thin stream, and check seasoning. Pour an appropriate amount over the spinach and onion and toss to combine.

**GROUPER**
Coat the fish fillets with the grapeseed oil and season with salt and pepper.

Spray the grill rack with nonstick spray and place the fish on the rack, skin side down. Shut the grill and cook for 2 to 3 minutes.

Open the grill and brush the fish with a layer of sauce. Cook for an additional 1 to 2 minutes. Repeat this procedure until the fish is cooked through.

Serve with or over the spinach salad.

**CARIBBEAN BBQ SAUCE**
1 CUP MANGO JUICE OR NECTAR
¼ CUP APRICOT PRESERVES
2 TEASPOONS LIME ZEST
2 TABLESPOONS FRESH-SQUEEZED LIME
  JUICE
3 TABLESPOONS HONEY
2 TEASPOONS FRESH GINGER, MINCED
1 TEASPOON GROUND CUMIN
¼ TEASPOON GROUND CINNAMON
1 JALAPEÑO PEPPER, SEEDED AND MINCED
PINCH OF SALT

**SPINACH SALAD**
2 TABLESPOONS WHITE WINE VINEGAR
1 TABLESPOON HONEY
¼ TEASPOON PAPRIKA
1 TEASPOON POPPY SEEDS
PINCH OF SALT
6 TABLESPOONS GRAPESEED OIL
1 BUNCH SPINACH, WELL-RINSED AND
  TORN INTO BITE-SIZE PIECES
½ SWEET ONION, THINLY SLICED

**GROUPER**
2 TABLESPOONS GRAPESEED OIL
1½ TO 2 POUNDS FRESH GROUPER FILLETS
SALT AND PEPPER, TO TASTE
NONSTICK COOKING SPRAY (FOR GRILL)

Curieux's complex flavor and long finish plead for strong, savory pairings to contrast its coconut, vanilla, and sweet bourbon character. A thin-crust pie like this one is just such an example. The crispy dough, light garlic, and salt from the feta cheese do a great balancing act with the beer's inherent oak tones, high ABV (11%), and lightly soured fruit notes. Plus, it's beer and pizza; you can't miss.

## Chicken Sausage Pizza

Preheat oven to 425°F.

In a small bowl, mix the ¼ cup of olive oil with a teaspoon of minced garlic and set aside.

Briefly wilt the spinach in a saucepan, adding a bit of oil or water to help it break down a bit (covering the saucepan will speed the process). Remove once wilted.

In a small bowl, pour the 2 teaspoons of olive oil and add the pizza dough, rotating the dough to make sure it is lightly coated. Cover the bowl with plastic wrap and let rise until dough has roughly doubled in size—or until the dough does not spring back when poked with a finger.

Using your hands, stretch the dough in the desired shape—mine looked like an uneven rectangle.

Spread the garlic and oil evenly across the surface of the dough.

Distribute the wilted spinach in small patches across the dough, then add the sliced chicken sausage, crumbled feta, and grated Parmesan.

Bake for about 20 minutes, either on a pizza stone or a seasoned sheet tray.

Garnish with sun-dried tomatoes, chopped basil, and another drizzle of olive oil.

16 OUNCES PIZZA DOUGH (FRESH OR FROZEN), AT ROOM TEMPERATURE
¼ CUP + 2 TEASPOONS OLIVE OIL
2 CLOVES OF GARLIC, MINCED
3 OUNCES SPINACH, STEAMED/WILTED
8 OUNCES ALREADY-COOKED CHICKEN SAUSAGE, SLICED THIN (¼-INCH)
6 OUNCES FETA CHEESE, CRUMBLED
4 OUNCES GRATED PARMESAN CHEESE
6 SUN-DRIED TOMATOES (REHYDRATED IF THEY AREN'T ALREADY IN OIL), CHOPPED FINE
1 TABLESPOON FRESH CHOPPED BASIL, FOR GARNISH

In addition to being delicious with beer, grilled cheese occupies an important place in American gastronomy, and its inclusion in this collection was nearly mandatory. Here we keep the fillings simple but add an extra layer of savory with the cheddar bread and a little arugula. The bewitching flavors of the Curieux are dominant, getting a helping hand from the mildness of the bread and cheese— and the nostalgia is delicious. Note: Best eaten cut into four little triangles.

## DOUBLE CHEDDAR GRILLED CHEESE SANDWICH

Butter all the bread slices on one side with approximately 1 teaspoon per slice.

Heat up a large nonstick skillet over medium heat and place two slices, butter side down, in the pan.

Immediately divide the cheese between the bread slices and season with a pinch of salt and pepper and top with arugula.

Place the other buttered bread slices (butter side up) on top and cook until the bottom slice is nicely browned. Flip the sandwich over and do the same to the other side.

When the bread has browned and the cheese has melted, remove from the pan, cut into desired shapes and sizes, and serve immediately.

4 SLICES CHEDDAR BREAD (HOPEFULLY FROM A LOCAL BAKERY)
4 TEASPOONS BUTTER, AT ROOM TEMPERATURE
3 OUNCES EXCELLENT CHEDDAR CHEESE, THINLY SLICED
SALT AND PEPPER, TO TASTE
1 HANDFUL FRESH BABY ARUGULA

In small quantities this is a dessert; in larger quantities it's brunch—and it's great either way. The sweet and sour of the chutney makes a delicious companion for the Curieux's own complex, wood-tinged fruit bouquet. The silky-smooth 11% ABV of the Curieux helps with any sugary aftertaste (from the real maple syrup you've just put over the top?) and makes for awesome contemporary comfort food.

# Vanilla Buttermilk Waffles with Apple Chutney

**APPLE CHUTNEY**

In a saucepan, combine all the ingredients together and simmer for 5 to 10 minutes, or until everything is nearly soft. Cool slightly and serve, or conserve in the refrigerator.

**WAFFLES**

Preheat waffle iron.

In a mixing bowl, add the flour, baking soda, baking powder, and salt and whisk to combine. Add the sugar, vanilla bean scrapings, eggs, and buttermilk and whisk well; then whisk in the melted butter. Combine the flour mixture with the buttermilk mixture and mix until uniform.

Let sit at least an hour before using, or let mature overnight.

After cooking in a waffle iron, serve with the prepared chutney.

**APPLE CHUTNEY**
5 APPLES, PEELED, MEDIUM DICE
½ RED ONION, SMALL DICE
2 TABLESPOONS FRESH GINGER ROOT, PEELED AND GRATED
¼ CUP GOLDEN RAISINS
½ CUP APPLE CIDER VINEGAR
3 OUNCES LIGHT BROWN SUGAR
½ TEASPOON CRUSHED RED PEPPER FLAKE
¼ TEASPOON CINNAMON
¼ TEASPOON WHITE PEPPER
¼ TEASPOON GROUND CARDAMOM
⅛ TEASPOON NUTMEG

**WAFFLES**
3 CUPS FLOUR
2 TEASPOONS BAKING SODA
1 TABLESPOON BAKING POWDER
2 TEASPOONS SALT
3 TABLESPOONS SUGAR
1 VANILLA BEAN, SCRAPED
5 EGGS, BEATEN
3 CUPS BUTTERMILK
8 OUNCES BUTTER, MELTED

# CURIEUX

Allagash Curieux is made by aging our Tripel ale in Jim Beam bourbon barrels for six to eight weeks in our cold cellars. The aged beer is then blended back with a portion of fresh Tripel, which serves to polish the rough edges of the bourbon character. The resulting beer is incredibly smooth with soft coconut and vanilla notes, and hints of bourbon. The finish consists of a lingering warmth and leaves you wanting more. A dangerously easy to drink 11% ABV makes Curieux a great beer for sharing with good friends and family.

Description: Bourbon Barrel Aged Strong Ale
ABV: 11%
Profile: Dark Golden, Coconut, Bourbon, Vanilla
Serving Temperature: 40° to 50°F
Availability: Year-Round
Package: 750ml bottle, 5.17 gallon keg
Ideal Within: One Year

# interlude

In 2004, continuing to explore traditions in Belgian beer making, Allagash brewmaster Jason Perkins became interested in making a Belgian farmhouse, or *saison*-style, ale. Traditionally, this pale to reddish-colored ale was brewed during the cool months and then supplied to farmworkers during the summer harvest for refreshment, as partial payment for what was no doubt grueling work. Fortunately for the farmhands, the beers were of a gentler nature (3–3.5% ABV) than the Allagash interpretation (9.5% ABV), and fortunately for us, we can enjoy Interlude without the fifteen hours of backbreaking labor.

Allagash's Interlude is the unique product of traditional Belgian farmhouse yeast plus a house strain of Brettanomyces. While waiting out the lengthy fermentation associated with this particular farmhouse yeast, the brewers noticed an additional visitor to the beer. The beer had begun to take on new flavors, including pear, apricot, graham cracker, and bread crust. The brewers knew, almost immediately, that the beer had inadvertently been exposed to a strain of Brettanomyces, a wild yeast found in the air. Never ones to back down from a challenge, the brewers embraced this change and began to think of new ways to enhance these flavors. The brewing team loved the myriad of flavors that the "Brett" was creating.

Since the success of Curieux, the brewers had been looking for an opportunity to continue to experiment with barrels. Rob called his friends at Plumpjack Winery in Napa Valley, California, and sourced some amazing wine barrels that had aged both Syrah and Merlot. Upon receiving the barrels, the brewers added the beer and waited. The results were better than they could have hoped. The beer gained complexity, a vinous plum character, and a drying, almost tannic and quite wine-like finish.

Interlude is a tireless partner around the table, going especially well with meats, whether cured, grilled, or smoked, as well as with bolder cheeses. The grilled chicken n' cheddar salad and spicy bacon chili meatloaf are particularly fancied, and the rosemary vanilla cream puffs steer the palate in another delicious direction entirely.

The rich flavors of venison embellished by a fresh cranberry relish are a suitable match for the wide-ranging flavors and taste experiences that come from drinking an Allagash Interlude: a virtual attack of vinous fruit, yeast, malt, spice, traces of earth, oak, and bread. Venison tenderloins aren't huge, so you'd better make this an appetizer, but bring out your big beer glasses.

# Venison Tenderloin with Spiced Cranberry Relish

## RELISH

In a saucepan, combine the water and sugar and bring to a boil over medium heat.

Add the cranberries, apples, cider vinegar, currants, and spices and return to a boil. Reduce heat and simmer gently for approximately 10 minutes. Pour the mixture into a bowl and place plastic wrap directly on the surface of the sauce.

Cool to room temperature and serve, or cover and refrigerate—bring relish to room temperature before serving.

## VENISON

Preheat oven to 300°F.

Coat the tenderloins with about three-quarters of the olive oil, half the thyme, and salt and pepper.

In a sauté pan, sear the venison tenderloins on each side, then continue cooking in the oven until the preferred temperature is reached. Let rest for about 5 minutes before serving with the relish.

Toss the sliced apple in the remaining olive oil and a pinch of the remaining thyme. Grill or sear them very briefly—just enough to add color and flavor.

Season the rested meat with the remaining thyme and cooked apple slices. Serve with the cranberry relish.

### RELISH
1 CUP WATER
1 CUP SUGAR
12 OUNCES FRESH CRANBERRIES
 (1 PACKAGE)
1 CUP APPLE, MEDIUM DICE
½ CUP APPLE CIDER VINEGAR
½ CUP DRIED CURRANTS
½ TEASPOON GROUND CINNAMON
¼ TEASPOON GROUND GINGER
¼ TEASPOON GROUND ALLSPICE
⅛ TEASPOON GROUND CLOVES

### VENISON
3 POUNDS VENISON TENDERLOINS
1½ TABLESPOONS OLIVE OIL
SALT AND PEPPER, TO TASTE
1 TEASPOON FRESH THYME, FINELY
 CHOPPED
1 APPLE, CORED AND MEDIUM SLICED

This salad dressing is actually the by-product of mixing a few great ingredients together. Instead of combining the lemon juice and oil into a vinaigrette-style dressing, they are left to their own devices. The combination of the strong character of the other ingredients and the great barrage of flavors from the Interlude makes for exciting eating! (I especially like the cheddar cheese—thanks Davina!)

# GRILLED CHICKEN N' CHEDDAR SALAD

**CHICKEN**
Preheat grill to 300°F.

In a measuring cup, add the olive oil, salt, and pepper and mix thoroughly, then separate 1 ounce for basting. Toss the chicken thighs in oil mixture and then place them on a grill over medium heat. Cook each side for 6 to 8 minutes.

After the first few minutes of the second side, brush with just a bit of the separated olive oil mixture every couple of minutes until they're fully cooked—160°F.

Let the chicken thighs cool for 5 minutes and brush with any remaining olive oil.

**CHEDDAR SALAD**
Set aside the romaine and arugula.

Place the rest of the ingredients in a large bowl and toss gently to mix; add the greens on top and gently fold over a couple of times to mix through.

Serve in a large bowl or on plates.

**CHICKEN**
8 OUNCES GRILLED CHICKEN, SHREDDED
3 OUNCES EXCELLENT OLIVE OIL
SEA SALT AND PEPPER, TO TASTE

**CHEDDAR SALAD**
6 TO 8 ROMAINE LEAVES, PICKED AND
    CLEANED
1 CUP ARUGULA, WASHED

1 MEDIUM GRANNY SMITH APPLE, CORED
    AND THINLY SLICED
3 SCALLIONS, TRIMMED AND THINLY
    SLICED
1 TO 2 ROASTED RED BELL PEPPERS
    (JARRED IS FINE), MEDIUM CHOPPED
¼ CUP GRAPESEED OIL
4 TEASPOONS FRESH SQUEEZED LEMON
    JUICE
3 SPRIGS THYME, CHOPPED FINE
4 OUNCES EXCELLENT CHEDDAR CHEESE,
    SHAVED
½ CUP PECANS, GENTLY TOASTED
SALT AND PEPPER TO TASTE

I always consider myself lucky when I get to eat smoked meats, and this dish does not disappoint. The doubly-yeasted, wood-tinged nose of the Allagash Interlude plays well with the smoky-sweet tang of the pork, and the strength of the mustard sauce holds up well against the unique and complex palate of the Interlude. And it's delicious.

# SMOKED PORK TENDERLOIN WITH KALE AND SWEET MUSTARD SAUCE

## PORK
Season the pork with salt and pepper. In a smoker, smoke the pork until the internal temperature is 145°F. Let rest 5 to 10 minutes before serving.

## KALE
Bring 2 quarts of salted water to a boil, then add a bay leaf and half the rosemary. Reduce the heat and let simmer for a few minutes. Rinse and pick the kale leaves from the stem, tearing them into bite-sized pieces.

Place all the kale in the salted water at once. Cook until bright green, about 1 minute. Strain the kale and cool under cold water; squeeze to dry.

In a sauté pan, over medium-high heat, add the olive oil and cook the onion for about 1 minute, or until translucent. Increase heat to high, add the kale to the pan, and then add the white wine. Reduce the wine a bit, then finish with butter and season to taste.

Serve with the sliced pork.

## SWEET MUSTARD SAUCE
Bring the vinegar, sugar, and Worcestershire sauce to a boil. Cut heat to simmer and reduce mixture by approximately one-third. Add the remaining ingredients (mustard, butter, lemon juice, and cayenne pepper) and simmer for about 10 minutes, adjusting consistency. Check seasoning and serve over the pork.

## PLATING
Slice the pork tenderloin into slices about ½ inch thick. Place a small pile of kale in the middle of the plate and arrange the pork around the kale. Spoon the mustard sauce over the pork and garnish with chopped rosemary, parsley, and diced bacon.

**PORK**
2 PORK TENDERLOINS
SALT AND PEPPER

**KALE**
2 QUARTS SALTED WATER
2 BUNCHES KALE (ANY VARIETY), PICKED
  AND CLEANED
1 BAY LEAF
1 SPRIG FRESH ROSEMARY, FINELY
  CHOPPED
2 TABLESPOONS OLIVE OIL
¼ YELLOW ONION, DICED SMALL
2 TABLESPOONS WHITE WINE
2 OUNCES BUTTER
4 SLICES COOKED BACON, FINELY
  CHOPPED

**SWEET MUSTARD SAUCE**
½ CUP BALSAMIC VINEGAR
¼ CUP BROWN SUGAR
1 TABLESPOON WORCESTERSHIRE SAUCE
1 CUP DIJON MUSTARD
2 TABLESPOONS BUTTER
JUICE FROM HALF A LEMON
¼ TEASPOON CAYENNE PEPPER

I love meatloaf, spicy meatloaf even more, and leftover meatloaf the most. This recipe guarantees all three, unless there are more than eight people for dinner! The familiar sweetness of Heinz ketchup and tang of the spicy chili sauce give this meatloaf some kick, while the savory spinach-and-cheese middle keep, it in check. One taste-tester commented, "Best. Meatloaf. Ever."

# SPICY BACON-CHILI MEATLOAF

Preheat oven to 350°F.

Mix all meatloaf ingredients together until uniform and set aside.

Mix all filling ingredients together until uniform and set aside.

On parchment paper, spread meat mixture into a large rectangle, approximately 11 by 14 inches, then cover the top with the spinach filling. Roll the mixture up, jelly-roll style, using the parchment paper to help form. Place in a baking dish with the "seam" facing down.

Wrap the top of the meatloaf in bacon, slightly overlapping the slices. Bake for 30 minutes.

## SAUCE
In a mixing bowl, stir together sauce ingredients.

After meatloaf has baked for 30 minutes, remove from the oven. Pour half the sauce mixture over the meatloaf, spreading to coat, and bake an additional 30 minutes.

Pour over and spread most of the remaining sauce and bake an additional 15 minutes to set the sauce and finish cooking. The meatloaf is fully cooked through when it reaches about 165°F.

Once the meatloaf is fully cooked, remove from the oven and give a final brush of the sauce over the top. Allow it to rest for 15 minutes before serving.

**MEATLOAF**
3 POUNDS GROUND BEEF (80/20)
½ CUP BASIL, FINELY CHOPPED
2 TOMATOES, MEDIUM CHOPPED
1 CUP COOKED BACON, FINELY CHOPPED
1 YELLOW ONION, SMALL DICE
¾ CUP PANKO (JAPANESE) BREAD CRUMBS
2 EGGS, BEATEN
3 TEASPOONS SALT
1 TEASPOON GROUND PEPPER
1 POUND RAW SLICED BACON (FOR THE TOP OF THE LOAF)

**FILLING**
12 OUNCES SPINACH, STEAMED
1 TABLESPOON OLIVE OIL
1 TEASPOON GARLIC, MINCED
½ CUP GRATED MOZZARELLA CHEESE (OR ABOUT 8 SLICES MEDIUM CHOPPED, IF FRESH)
4 OUNCES GRATED PARMESAN CHEESE
1 TEASPOON FRESH THYME, FINELY CHOPPED
¼ TEASPOON SALT

**SAUCE**
1 CUP HEINZ KETCHUP
1 CUP SPICY CHILI SAUCE (LIKE SRIRACHA)
1 TABLESPOON WORCESTERSHIRE SAUCE
1 TABLESPOON FRESH-SQUEEZED LEMON JUICE
2 TEASPOONS DIJON MUSTARD

Rosemary grows all over northern California, and it ends up in my kitchen a lot. In this variation of the iconic cream puff, the invigorating bite of fresh rosemary gives an edge to the warmth of vanilla bean and makes for a sweet treat that holds its own against the waves of flavor from Allagash Interlude.

# Rosemary Vanilla Cream Puffs

### ROSEMARY VANILLA PASTRY CREAM

In a saucepan, combine the heavy cream, half the sugar, vanilla bean or seeds, rosemary, and salt. Bring just about to a simmer and turn off the heat (avoid boiling).

In a mixing bowl, add the egg yolks, remaining sugar, and cornstarch and whisk together to combine. Still whisking, slowly pour the hot cream mixture into the egg yolk mixture, a little at a time until incorporated. Pour mixture back into saucepan and cook over medium-high heat until it thickens (160°F). Remove and discard the vanilla bean.

Transfer the mixture to the bowl of an electric mixer fitted with the paddle attachment. On medium speed, add the butter and beat the mixture for a few minutes to cool. Cover with plastic wrap directly on the surface of the pastry cream (it prevents a skin from forming while it cools) and refrigerate until chilled—a few hours. Whisk before serving for a smooth texture.

### PUFF PASTRY DOUGH

Preheat oven to 375°F.

In a saucepan, combine milk, water, butter, and salt and bring just to a boil. Remove from heat and add all the flour at once, stirring quickly with a spatula or wooden spoon to incorporate.

When all the flour has been incorporated, return the pan over medium heat and cook for another minute or two, stirring to prevent the dough from browning. Transfer the dough from the pan to the bowl of a mixer. Beat with paddle on low speed for a few seconds, then add eggs one at a time, fully incorporating each one before adding the next.

Prepare a baking sheet. Using a pastry bag, pipe out approximately 2-inch mounds of dough with a couple of inches between each one (they will expand during baking). Whisk together 1 egg and 2 tablespoons of water and brush each mound of dough with the mixture. Bake for 25 to 30 minutes, rotating baking sheets while cooking to ensure even color. Let cool before serving. You may also freeze them for future use—when ready to use, just put them in a hot oven for a few minutes to crisp them up.

## TO ASSEMBLE

If you own a bismark tube (special long-nosed design for filling pastry), use that as the tip on the pastry bag and fill from the bottom. If you do not own a bismark tube, make a small slit in the side of the puff and fill from the side with a small standard pastry tip.

**ROSEMARY VANILLA PASTRY CREAM**
2 CUPS HEAVY CREAM
½ CUP SUGAR, DIVIDED EVENLY
¼ VANILLA BEAN, SPLIT LENGTHWISE AND
   SCRAPED
1 TEASPOON FRESH ROSEMARY, FINELY
   CHOPPED
PINCH OF SALT
4 EGG YOLKS
¼ CUP CORNSTARCH
1½ TABLESPOONS UNSALTED BUTTER,
   ROOM TEMPERATURE

**PUFF PASTRY DOUGH**
¼ CUP MILK
¼ CUP + 2 TABLESPOONS WATER
6 OUNCES UNSALTED BUTTER (1½ STICKS)
½ TEASPOON SALT
2 PLUS CUPS FLOUR, SIFTED OR WHISKED
5 EGGS + 1 EGG

ALLAGASH

2011
september | interlude

ale aged in red wine barrels
with Brettanomyces

# interlude

Allagash Interlude is brewed with a base of pilsner malt and fermented using two distinctly different yeast strains. The first, a Belgian farmhouse yeast, establishes the flavor foundations of a classic Belgian-style ale. The second, a house strain of Brettanomyces yeast, contributes an intriguing myriad of flavors, including pear, apricot, graham cracker, and bread crust. This second yeast, which gives the Interlude its tremendous complexity, is a yeast strain that was discovered and cultured here at Allagash. An innovative brewing process, special fermentations, and French oak barrel aging all contribute to a beer of unparalleled complexity. After fermentation, a portion of the Interlude is aged in French Merlot and Syrah oak barrels, which impart a distinctive vinous, plum character and a drying, almost tannic finish.

Description: Farmhouse Ale aged in Wine Barrels
ABV: 9.5%
Profile: Red, Bready, Tropical Fruit, Slightly Tart
Serving Temperature: 40° to 50°F
Availability: Limited Annual Release
Package: 750ml bottle, 5.17 gallon keg
Ideal Within: Three Years

# CHAPTER 7

# black

Stouts have been around since the seventeenth century, growing up alongside and intertwined with the porter. However, a stout was not always a dark beer, but rather a strong one, the association of a darker color not becoming de rigeur until the nineteenth century. As the stout began to be popular in other locales, different interpretations emerged, produced in either a sweeter or drier style with an ABV range of 4 to 8%.

By 2007, Allagash had successfully tackled several of the traditional Belgian styles and had done a good deal of experimentation as well. One thing that it had not done was to put a Belgian twist on a beer not commonly associated with Belgium. Allagash Black was created by brewer Dee Dee Germain who, at the time, found herself in a dark beer phase. Having tried many stouts and Belgian beers, she loved the idea of merging the chocolate and roasted character of a stout and the fruitiness and complexity of a Belgian beer. Turns out it was not only a good idea, but a tasty one.

Pairing stouts is fairly easy, as they lend themselves to meats and sweets. There are other options, but starting in one of those categories is a good way to get a handle on a style that may otherwise be intimidating at first glance. Oatmeal cookies, lamb, sausages, and chocolate all pair well, or just an excellent vanilla ice cream. Better yet, put a scoop on top of the black chocolate bread pudding with a glass of Allagash Black. It might just end up as your dinner.

It's a humble recipe, but cottage pie goes royally well with the wheat, barley, and oats expressed in the Allagash Black and reflects the agrarian roots of both cooking and beer-making. The earthy, roasted character of this pairing is aided with sweet highlights from the onion and carrot, not to mention the healthy dose of candi sugar in the brew. You can call it shepherd's pie if you must, but a group of my English friends would have you know that one is made with lamb.

# COTTAGE PIE

Preheat oven to 400°F.

In a large pan, heat the grapeseed oil and briefly sauté the onion and carrot—about 1 minute. Add ground meats, mix thoroughly, and brown over high heat for 4 to 5 minutes. Add the salt and tomatoes and mix well. Reduce the heat and simmer lightly for 10 to 15 minutes. Remove meat mixture from heat and stir in chopped thyme, then set aside.

In salted water, cook the potatoes until they're cooked through (but not falling apart). Once cooked, strain and mash them with the butter and check seasoning.

Fill a large baking dish or cast-iron skillet with the meat mixture to halfway. Top with the mashed potatoes. Sprinkle the top with the farmer's cheese and bake at 400°F for about 20 minutes, or until the cheese has melted and browned a bit.

Let stand for at least 10 minutes before serving.

2 TABLESPOONS GRAPESEED OIL
1 YELLOW ONION, SMALL DICE
1 CARROT, SMALL DICE
¾ POUND GROUND BEEF
¾ POUND GROUND PORK
1 POUND TOMATOES, DICED (CANNED ARE OK)
2 TEASPOONS FRESH THYME, FINELY CHOPPED
1½ TEASPOONS SALT
GROUND PEPPER, TO TASTE
3 POUNDS RUSSET POTATOES, PEELED AND MEDIUM DICE
8 OUNCES BUTTER, ROOM TEMPERATURE
4 OUNCES FARMER'S CHEESE

Allagash Black's roasted grain, coffee, and dark chocolate notes give it a stout flavor profile while its crisp, clean finish makes it a great beer to pair with foods. I especially like what happens with the rich, distinct flavors of lamb. In this recipe the dried herbs/oil, lamb, and the Black share broad, dark, and savory qualities aided by the flavors of a grill. They taste great together and help make the peppers and pesto all the brighter.

# GRILLED LAMB CHOPS WITH WHITE BEANS AND MINT PESTO

**WHITE BEANS** *(Start at least 6 hours ahead of time.)*

In a large mixing bowl, add the dried white beans (of your choosing) and set aside. In a saucepan, bring the water, rosemary, and bay leaf to a boil and then pour over the beans. Let stand approximately 6 hours or overnight.

After the beans have soaked, finish cooking on the stove at medium heat, adding water if necessary to keep the beans in plenty of liquid. Drain the beans, reserving some of the cooking liquid, and set both aside.

In a saucepan, over medium heat, add the butter and shallot and sauté for about a minute. Add the beans and a bit of the reserved cooking liquid and cook until the beans are heated through. Add the chopped parsley and salt and pepper; check seasoning and serve.

**LAMB CHOPS**
Preheat and prepare grill.

In a mixing bowl, toss the lamb chops in the olive oil, oregano, thyme, rosemary, and salt and pepper. Set aside.

Grill the lamb for about 4 minutes a side (for medium rare). Let rest a few minutes before serving with the white beans and mint pesto.

**MINT PESTO**
In a food processor, add the pine nuts and herbs, and pulse to roughly chop. Add the Parmesan cheese, salt, and pepper to the pine nut mixture; pulse quickly just to incorporate. Turn the food processor on and slowly add olive oil in a thin stream, quickening the pouring speed slightly as the mixture emulsifies. Adjust the seasoning and put in a storage container with a bit of additional olive oil. Cover with plastic wrap over the surface to preserve the fresh green color. Conserve in the refrigerator.

**LAMB**
2 POUNDS LAMB LOIN CHOPS
  (APPROXIMATELY 8 TO 10 CHOPS)
2 TABLESPOONS OLIVE OIL
1 TEASPOON DRIED OREGANO
1 TEASPOON DRIED THYME
1 TEASPOON DRIED ROSEMARY
1 TEASPOON SALT
½ TEASPOON FRESHLY GROUND BLACK
  PEPPER

**WHITE BEANS**
3 QUARTS WATER
2 CUPS WHITE BEANS, DRIED
2 OUNCES BUTTER
1 MEDIUM SHALLOT, FINE DICE
1 TO 2 TABLESPOONS FLAT-LEAF PARSLEY,
  CHOPPED
½ TEASPOON SALT
FRESHLY GROUND PEPPER, TO TASTE

**MINT PESTO**
2 CLOVES GARLIC, ROUGHLY CHOPPED
¼ CUP PINE NUTS
¾ CUP FRESH BASIL, LIGHTLY PACKED
1½ CUPS FRESH MINT
¾ CUP FLAT-LEAF PARSLEY
½ CUP GRATED PARMESAN CHEESE
½ TEASPOON SALT
½ TEASPOON FRESHLY GROUND BLACK
  PEPPER
¾ CUP EXCELLENT OLIVE OIL

I really couldn't see a way around including a burger in a beer pairing book. Then I stopped wanting to find one. Burgers are iconic in the States—oh, and really good with beer. In this recipe, the distinct sweet-smoke of the chipotle pepper, savory cheddar, and salty bacon are made even more fine by the chocolate-malt of Allagash Black. Like a half-pound of cheese-covered Americana, Allagash Black doesn't get tired.

# Chipotle Bacon Burger

Preheat grill.

In a mixing bowl, combine the ground beef, adobo sauce, garlic, salt, and pepper.

Mix thoroughly by hand until the consistency is uniform and let rest for 15 minutes.

Slice cheese; cook off bacon; toast or briefly grill the inside of each bun.

Form into 4 to 6 patties and cook each to the desired temperature.

2 POUNDS LEAN GROUND BEEF
2½ TABLESPOONS ADOBO SAUCE
2 TEASPOONS SALT
1 TEASPOON FRESHLY GROUND PEPPER
1½ TEASPOONS GARLIC, MINCED
2 TABLESPOONS GRAPESEED OIL
3 TO 4 OUNCES EXCELLENT CHEDDAR
  CHEESE, THINLY SLICED
8 STRIPS COOKED BACON

This hearty dish was actually designed to pull on the refined side of Allagash Black. Dark beers aren't always celebrated for their more delicate nuances; neither is chili. But this particular chili stays on the lighter side of the taste and spice spectrum, and the tomato, coffee, earth, and savory qualities overlap in the Black. The blue cheese and gougeres make it that much more aromatic.

# BUFFALO CHILI WITH BLUE CHEESE GOUGERES

## CHILI

In a heavy-bottom stockpot, over medium heat, heat the chili flakes, cumin, chili powder, coriander, and paprika in the grapeseed oil until fragrant. Add the onions and garlic and cook for about 1 minute, then add the meat and brown well. Add all other ingredients and simmer for another couple hours, stirring occasionally. Check seasoning, garnish with crumbled blue cheese, scallions, cilantro, and hot sauce, and serve with gougeres.

## GOUGERES

Preheat oven to 375°F.

In a saucepan, combine milk, water, butter, and salt and bring just to a boil. Remove from heat and add all the flour at once, stirring quickly with a spatula or wooden spoon to incorporate. When all the flour has been incorporated, return the pan to the burner, cooking for another 2 to 3 minutes, stirring to prevent the dough from browning.

Transfer the dough from the pan to a mixer and beat with paddle on low speed for a few seconds. Turn the mixer speed to medium and add eggs, one at a time, fully incorporating each one before adding the next. Turn the mixer speed to the lowest setting and add blue cheese and salt and pepper.

Using a pastry bag, pipe out approximately 2-inch mounds of dough with a couple inches between each one—they will expand during baking.

Whisk together 1 egg and 2 tablespoons of water and brush each gougere with the mixture. Then crack some black pepper over the top.

Bake for about 15 to 20 minutes, rotating baking sheets while cooking to ensure even color. Depending on the size you make, they may take longer.

Remove from oven when nicely browned and let cool before serving.

## CHILI
3 TABLESPOONS GRAPESEED OIL
2 TEASPOONS RED CHILI PEPPER FLAKES
1 TEASPOON CUMIN POWDER
2 TEASPOONS CHILI POWDER
1 TEASPOON CORIANDER
2 TEASPOONS PAPRIKA
1 TEASPOON SMOKED PAPRIKA
1 YELLOW ONION, MEDIUM DICE
3 TABLESPOONS MINCED GARLIC
1½ POUNDS COARSELY GROUND BUFFALO
1 CUP RED WINE
½ CUP STRONG BLACK COFFEE
3 CANS TOMATOES (14-OUNCE EACH),
  DICED, WHOLE, OR CHOPPED
2 TEASPOONS SALT
½ TEASPOON WHITE PEPPER
1 BAY LEAF
EXTRA WATER FOR CONSISTENCY

## GOUGERES
¾ CUP MILK
¾ CUP + 2 TABLESPOONS WATER
6 OUNCES UNSALTED BUTTER
¾ TEASPOON SALT
½ TEASPOON FRESHLY GROUND PEPPER
12 OUNCES FLOUR, SIFTED OR WHISKED
5 LARGE EGGS
1 CUP BLUE CHEESE, CRUMBLED
1 EGG

## GARNISHES
CRUMBLED BLUE CHEESE
4 TABLESPOONS FRESH CILANTRO, FINELY
  CHOPPED
2 SCALLIONS, THINLY SLICED
HOT SAUCE

Black is always in fashion in the Northeast, especially when we take Allagash's wildly popular ale and make it part of a classic dessert—bread pudding. Combined with bittersweet chocolate, vanilla, and shaved nutmeg this Black bread pudding will open your eyes to the versatility of dark beer and that loaf of bread.

# BLACK CHOCOLATE BREAD PUDDING

Preheat oven to 325°F.

Set up a double boiler, or a bowl over simmering water, to evenly melt chocolate. Set aside.

In a saucepan, gently heat the milk and Allagash Black to a simmer, then pour over the chocolate. Let sit for 1 minute, then whisk slowly until uniform. Set aside to cool.

Cube bread into bite-sized pieces, place in a mixing bowl, and set aside.

In another mixing bowl, whisk the eggs, sugar, nutmeg, and vanilla until slightly frothy; then slowly pour in the milk mixture. Pour the egg-milk mixture over the cubed bread, making sure all of them have absorbed some of the liquid.

Prepare a 9-by-13-inch baking dish with nonstick spray, then transfer the bread-egg mixture to the dish, spreading evenly. Sprinkle some extra sugar over the top. Cover the baking dish with foil, then place in a larger roasting pan to prepare for a water bath. To lessen the chance of spilling, place roasting pan (with the baking dish) in the oven before adding water for the water bath. Fill the roasting pan with water until it reaches about three-quarters of the way up the sides of the baking dish.

Bake for 30 to 35 minutes; then check every 5 minutes until done. (The sides will pull away from the dish a little bit and the center will be fairly firm when pressed.)

Sprinkle with a few additional chocolate chips and let cool for 10 minutes before serving (hopefully with vanilla bean gelato).

½ CUP BITTERSWEET CHOCOLATE CHIPS, PLUS MORE FOR GARNISHING
2 CUPS WHOLE MILK
¾ CUP ALLAGASH BLACK
12 TO 14 OUNCES BREAD, CUT IN SMALL CUBES
4 EGGS
2 CUPS SUGAR (PLUS A LITTLE EXTRA FOR SPRINKLING)
1 TEASPOON PURE VANILLA EXTRACT
¼ TEASPOON FRESHLY GRATED NUTMEG
1 TO 2 QUARTS HOT WATER (WATER BATH)

# black

belgian
style
stout

# black

Allagash Black is brewed with 2 Row barley, torrified wheat, oats, both roasted and chocolate malts, and a generous portion of dark caramelized candi sugar. The beer is then fermented using a strain of yeast indigenous to the Flemish region of Belgium, adding a layer of complex fruitiness. The silky mouthfeel is a great balance to the roasted character and coffee and dark chocolate notes expressed throughout this beer.

Description: Belgian-Style Stout
ABV: 7.5%
Profile: Dark, Roasted, Chocolate
Serving Temperature: 40°to 50°F
Availability: Year-Round
Package: 12oz bottle, 750ml bottle, 5.17 gallon keg, and 15.5 gallon keg
Ideal Within: One Year

# CHAPTER 8

# Victoria Ale

Portland, Maine's rich history is evidenced by numerous attractions around the city—lighthouses, forts, museums, the Old Port, and the Victoria Mansion. Also known as the Morse-Libby House and designed by architect Henry Austin, it survives as a unique example of the princely palaces created for America's wealthiest citizens in the pre–Civil War era and continues to offer its charms to modern-day visitors in the form of a museum.

While the term *Victorian* has not always been associated with beer, it became so in Portland after a representative from the Victoria Mansion called Allagash to see if it would brew a beer in honor of the historic landmark. Intrigued, the brewing team visited the mansion to have a look around; after seeing several visual references to Bacchus, the Thracian God of Wine, the brewers decided to brew a beer with grapes, but using a strain of yeast usually reserved for wine. Victoria was born and was the first beer in the Allagash Tribute series of beers, allowing the brewery to give back to the Portland community.

Fusing the worlds of beer and wine, two hundred pounds of Chardonnay grapes were brought in, crushed on site, and added directly to the mash. Victoria Ale's aroma is fruity spice with subtle notes of green banana, black pepper, and fresh-crushed mint. With a focus on the subtle wine-like character of the grapes, the 9.0% ABV beer is a pale copper color with Belgian yeast influences and a medium body. The finish is a long one, full of candied fruit, hints of honeydew melon, and white wine grapes.

For the home chef, the elegant strength of the Victoria Ale is versatile. It aligns effortlessly with subtle flavors, as in the corn-fried oysters, but has no trouble extending its character to heartier dishes, such as the Twenty-First-Century Pot Roast. While a light-colored ale might not be a clear choice for richer dishes, don't let the color fool you; much like the beer's namesake, it's incredibly refined yet has plenty of backbone.

These breaded oysters are the result of drinking my first glass of Victoria at 10:30 in the morning in Portland, Maine. I kept thinking how I wanted oysters with this beer—and this is the outcome. Coarse-ground cornmeal provides a great texture, and the cayenne pepper provides kick. The slight heat and crunch play well with the subtle fruit and spice notes from the Victoria, but don't be fooled by her well-balanced flavor profile—Victoria still rules. A 9% ABV and delightfully long finish keep her firmly on the throne.

## CORN-FRIED OYSTERS

Place the buttermilk in a small bowl, shuck the oysters into the buttermilk, and let them soak a few minutes.

In another bowl, add the cornmeal, flour, salt, paprika, sugar, and cayenne pepper and whisk to combine.

Drain oysters, then dredge well in the flour mixture and quick-fry on both sides in the oil at about 370°F until just browned.

Transfer to a paper towel, let drain for a few seconds, and serve right away.

12 FRESHLY SHUCKED OYSTERS
2 CUPS BUTTERMILK
¼ CUP GRAPESEED OIL
¾ CUP CORNMEAL
¼ CUP ALL-PURPOSE FLOUR
1 TEASPOON KOSHER SALT
1 TEASPOON PAPRIKA
½ TEASPOON SUGAR
½ TEASPOON CAYENNE PEPPER

Having lived in Tahoe for several years, I know the fish tacos at Sunnyside Restaurant on the north shore are a regular part of the local diet, and I had them in mind while creating this recipe. The brightness of the marinade and the perfect mild of the whitefish accentuated with the grill flavor show off the unripe banana and fresh ground pepper notes of the Victoria, while the sweet and spicy slaw, fresh cilantro, and lime all point to the minty, melon shades during the finish—totally refreshing in the merciless heat and humidity of a Southern summer.

# OPEN-FACED GRILLED SNAPPER TACOS

Preheat, clean, and season a grill.

**MARINADE**

In a mixing bowl, add the Allagash Victoria, lime juice, brown sugar, kosher salt, and scallions and whisk to combine. Reserve one-quarter of the marinade, placing the rest in a baking dish or resealable plastic bag, and add the snapper. Let sit for about 15 minutes, turning fish every so often.

**FILLING**

While the fish is marinating, combine the mayonnaise, vinegar, sugar, celery seed, and hot sauce (if you'd like) to make the dressing; then toss just enough with the cabbage and carrot to coat. Set aside.

On a well-seasoned grill, cook the fish through (just a few minutes on high heat), basting with the reserved marinade and sprinkling with a pinch of salt. Move to a plate and prepare to serve.

In a frying pan, heat about a tablespoon of the frying oil over high heat and flash-fry the tortillas, stacking them two per plate.

Divide the grilled fish among the tortillas, top with dressed cabbage, sliced avocado, and chopped cilantro. Spritz with lime juice and serve.

**MARINADE**
¼ CUP ALLAGASH VICTORIA
¼ CUP FRESHLY SQUEEZED LIME JUICE
1 TABLESPOON BROWN SUGAR
PINCH OF KOSHER SALT + SOME FOR
 SEASONING
1 SCALLION, THINLY SLICED

1 POUND FRESH RED SNAPPER (OR
 SIMILAR WHITEFISH)

**FILLING**
⅛ TO ¼ CUP HIGH-TEMP FRYING OIL
8 SOFT FLOUR OR CORN TORTILLAS (I
 LIKE BLUE CORN)
5 OUNCES MAYONNAISE
2 TABLESPOONS APPLE CIDER VINEGAR
1 TABLESPOON SUGAR
1 TEASPOON CELERY SEED
3 TO 4 DASHES OF HOT SAUCE (OPTIONAL)
¾ CUP SHREDDED RED CABBAGE
¾ CUP SHREDDED GREEN CABBAGE
¼ CUP SHREDDED CARROT
1 AVOCADO, THINLY SLICED
1 LIME, CUT INTO WEDGES

I don't think smoked foods require a lot to go with them, but a great beer definitely makes the list. The Victoria—refined and beautiful—is paired here with the steady heat and complex smoke flavors of baby back ribs and chile powder. The way the two flavor profiles balance each other is a pinpoint example of opposites attracting. And together they create something new entirely.

# ANCHO-RUBBED BABY BACK RIBS

Preheat the smoker, aiming for about 325°F.

In a mixing bowl, whisk together all the spices, then transfer to a spice shaker or fine sieve.

Using a shaker or fine strainer well above the meat, sprinkle the dry rub over the ribs on all sides in an even fashion (the extra height helps the spices settle more evenly); after all the surface is covered, give them another quick dusting and put them in the smoker.

Smoke the ribs at 325° to 350°F for about 2 hours, or until the meat on the edge of the ribs will peel cleanly from the bone and the racks droop heavily when held straight across.

When the ribs are cooked through, remove from heat and brush with a layer of sauce.

Wrap the sauced ribs in plastic wrap, or place in an airtight container, and steam them for 15 minutes.

Unwrap the ribs and put on a plate or platter. Brush them again with barbecue sauce and serve immediately.

4½ POUNDS BABY BACK PORK RIBS
ONE 18-OUNCE BOTTLE QUALITY
  BARBECUE SAUCE

**DRY RUB MIXTURE**
3 TABLESPOONS ANCHO CHILI POWDER
1 TABLESPOON KOSHER SALT
1 TABLESPOON BLACK PEPPER
1 TABLESPOON ONION POWDER
1 TABLESPOON GARLIC POWDER

Equal parts comfort food and nostalgia, a pot roast usually produces smiles and nods of agreement around tables throughout the country, and certainly in my native Ohio. In this dish the unique aromatic qualities of fennel and parsnip help highlight some of the complexities of the Victoria. Cured black olives provide a little snap to complement the otherwise still traditional flavors of the roast. My grandmothers would be proud, I hope; but if not, neither one was much of a cook!

# Twenty-First-Century Pot Roast

Preheat oven to 350°F.

In a mixing bowl, add the coriander, cumin, fennel seeds, and salt and pepper and mix well. Liberally season the roast. Place an ovenproof roasting pan on the stove with high heat and add the first 2 tablespoons of olive oil. When hot, brown the roast well on all sides, then remove from the pan and set aside.

To the roasting pan, add half the onion, bay leaf, garlic, dried thyme, and dried rosemary. Mix together and sauté for approximately 5 minutes or until onions begin to brown slightly. Add beef broth, wine, and half the olives, and bring the mixture to a boil, then place the roast back in the pan.

Cover the pan and place in oven. Cook for 2 hours, checking the liquid every 30 minutes, adding a bit of water if necessary—but the goal is to reduce the amount of liquid to develop flavor. After 2 hours, check the liquid level again, uncover, and reduce the heat to 300°F. Continue to cook the roast until it is done (when fully cooked it shreds easily with a fork).

While the beef is roasting, in a mixing bowl, add the remaining onion, carrots, parsnips, and fennel. Add the other 2 tablespoons of olive oil, a pinch of salt and pepper, and 2 tablespoons of the fresh chopped herbs and toss to mix well. Spread the vegetable mixture over baking trays and roast for about 15 minutes, or until the vegetables begin to brown. Remove from the oven to let cool.

When the roast is finished, remove roasting pan from the oven, cover, and let it rest for 20 to 30 minutes before serving. While the roast is resting, reheat roasted vegetables in the oven for a few minutes along with the remaining olives. Serve with the roast and braising liquid.

**CHEF'S NOTE**

If you wish, a quick sauce can be made:

Strain the liquid from the roasting pan, replacing the cover to let the roast rest. Combine 1 tablespoon flour with 1 tablespoon butter and place in a saucepan over medium heat, cooking until a sweet, toasted aroma is emitted from the flour. Then add the roasting liquid while whisking constantly. Simmer until the mixture thickens and adjust the consistency with additional broth or water as the volume of juice remaining will vary. Check seasoning and adjust if necessary.

Chop the remaining fresh herbs (thyme and rosemary) and add to the sauce, or use them to garnish the serving dish.

3- TO 4-POUND BONELESS CHUCK ROAST
½ TEASPOON GROUND CORIANDER
½ TEASPOON GROUND CUMIN
1 TEASPOON WHOLE FENNEL SEEDS
1 TABLESPOON SALT
2 TEASPOONS FRESHLY GROUND BLACK PEPPER
2 TABLESPOONS + 2 TABLESPOONS OLIVE OIL, SEPARATED
1 YELLOW ONION, LARGE DICE
1 BAY LEAF
3 CLOVES GARLIC, MINCED
1 TEASPOON DRIED THYME
½ TEASPOON DRIED ROSEMARY
1 QUART BEEF BROTH
1 CUP RED WINE
1 CUP OIL-CURED BLACK OLIVES, ROUGHLY CHOPPED

3 MEDIUM CARROTS, LARGE DICE
2 PARSNIPS, LARGE DICE
2 FENNEL BULBS, LARGE DICE
2 TEASPOONS + 1 TEASPOON FRESH THYME, CHOPPED FINE
2 TEASPOONS + 1 TEASPOON FRESH ROSEMARY, CHOPPED FINE

This wonderful cake with big flavor is accented by richly flavored dried plums, and a slow-cooking water bath creates luxurious texture. Brown sugar and ginger provide a potent pique of spice that accents the aromas of banana, melon, and grape from the Victoria. A variation on a variation of a cake from Bar Agricole in San Francisco!

## GINGER PLUM CAKE

Preheat oven to 325°F.

Coat your 8- to 9-inch springform pan in butter and sugar and coat the underside with a double sheeting of aluminum foil to protect against leakage.

In a saucepan, bring the water to a boil, add plums and brandy, and simmer for 5 minutes. Remove from heat, stir in baking soda, and let mixture rest for 20 minutes.

Whisk together flour, baking powder, ginger, and salt, then set aside.

With a mixer, cream butter, sugar, and salt (this takes several minutes), then scrape the edges of the bowl. Add eggs, one at a time, fully incorporating one before adding the next, then scrape the bowl again. Add the flour mixture in two additions on the lowest speed, scraping and folding the mixture between each batch. Keeping the mixer speed on low, add the water-plum mixture and mix until uniform.

Pour into prepared springform and bake in a water bath for approximately 50 minutes, or until a toothpick inserted near the sides (which cook last in a water bath) comes out clean, and the edges pull back from the pan a bit.

Let cool and serve.

2½ CUPS WATER
1¼ CUPS DRIED PLUMS (PRUNES), PITTED
  AND CHOPPED COARSELY
¼ CUP BRANDY, BURNED OFF

2½ CUPS ALL-PURPOSE FLOUR
1¾ TEASPOONS BAKING SODA
½ TEASPOON + ⅛ TEASPOON BAKING
  POWDER
2 TEASPOONS GROUND GINGER

4 OUNCES BUTTER (ROOM
  TEMPERATURE), PLUS A SMALL
  AMOUNT FOR BAKING DISH
1 CUP PACKED BROWN SUGAR
½ TEASPOON + ⅛ TEASPOON SALT
4 EGGS

2012

*Victoria Ale*

# ALLAGASH

*Ale Brewed with White Grapes*

9% Alc. By Vol.

OPEN CAUTIOUSLY: CONTENTS UNDER PRESSURE

1 PINT 9.4 FL OZ (750 ML)

*Victoria Ale*

Allagash Victoria is brewed using a blend of classic brewing barley and New England–grown, white wine grapes. It then undergoes a fermentation using a wine yeast. The use of both wine grapes and a wine yeast, of course, makes the finished product end up somewhere between a wine and a beer. The traditional malt character of the beer is the backdrop to the delicate fruit profile asserted by the wine grapes. Victoria's long, dry finish is sure to leave you wanting more.

Description: Belgian Strong Ale Brewed with White Grapes
ABV: 9%
Profile: Golden, Fresh Cucumber, Vinous, Slight Pepper
Serving Temperature: 40° to 50°F
Availability: Limited Annual Release
Package: 750ml bottle, 5.17 gallon keg
Ideal Within: Two Years

# CHAPTER 9

# Hugh Malone

IPA, or India Pale Ale, refers to a hop-forward style of English pale ale that was popularized throughout the nineteenth century for shipment to consumers in India. This particular style eventually became prevalent in England, and by 1900, IPAs were being brewed in the United States, Canada, and Australia. More recently in the United States the India Pale Ale has enjoyed a renaissance, with dozens of excellent examples being offered by breweries around the country. Hop quantity and intensity were features of a competitive marketplace, but brewers eventually relaxed into more artful expressions. Almost obligatory for craft brewers from coast to coast, aficionados can afford to be picky with IPAs as they are nearly ubiquitous. Along with the bright, herbal aromas comes a medium-body, refreshing bitterness and lip-smackingly malty sweetness.

Although Belgian beers aren't known as being particularly hoppy, Allagash employees and locals had a thirst for hops, and the brewery all-too-happily wanted to expand the boundaries of Belgian-inspired beers. Hugh Malone, with an ABV of 7.8%, emerged as a Belgian-style IPA. It was named after one of the compounds in hops that provides coveted bitterness, the humulone, or Hugh Malone. A blend of hops is used throughout the brewing process, providing the necessary bitterness, a complex floral aroma, and a dry finish. Along with the refined texture resulting from Allagash's bottle conditioning, Hugh Malone is a particularly complex and elegant example of the style, managing to heighten the aromas of the hops with the traditional fruitiness of Belgian yeast.

As well as being eminently drinkable, the Hugh Malone makes a fine table companion for a list of comfort foods like burgers or fish n' chips and its bitterness allows it to blend with spicy and heartier fare as well. Favorites in this chapter are the gumbo, pad thai, and the sea-salted caramels.

It doesn't take a chef to know that deep-fried cod with twice-fried potatoes and beer tastes great, but it does take a deep fryer, or a deep skillet and some courage. After the logistics are worked out, this combination of two New England specialties (cod and Allagash beer) more than makes up for the challenge. Hugh Malone, a Belgian take on the IPA style, adds a little refinement to an otherwise brawny combination.

# Hugh's Fish n' Chips

**BATTER**
In a mixing bowl, whisk the flour, kosher salt, baking powder, and cayenne pepper together and set aside.

In a separate, larger bowl, whisk together beer, olive oil, and dijon mustard. Gently mix in the flour mixture until uniform.

Using a hand or stand mixer, whisk the egg whites until stiff peaks form. Mix approximately one-quarter of the egg whites into the flour mixture to loosen it up a bit, then fold in the remaining whites until uniform. Let sit for about 20 minutes before using.

Place each piece of fish in the batter, remove, and place in a hot pan of oil or deep fryer cooking at a temperature of 360°F.

**CHIPS**
Preheat frying oil to 275°F.

Skin the potatoes and cut them into the desired size.

In smaller batches, fry the chips until they just start to dry out on the edges, but without browning (2 to 4 minutes depending on size). Remove from the oil, drain, and place on sheet trays lined with paper towels to absorb oil. Let cool for 15 to 20 minutes.

Increase fryer oil temperature to 375°F.

In similar-sized batches, fry the chips a second time until the desired brown is achieved—again, 2 to 4 minutes. Drain, then toss in a bowl with salt and pepper and serve, or keep warm in a 200°F oven.

3 POUNDS EXCELLENT COD

BATTER
3½ CUPS FLOUR
1 TABLESPOON KOSHER SALT
1 TEASPOON BAKING POWDER
¼ TEASPOON CAYENNE PEPPER
2 CUPS HUGH MALONE
1 OUNCE OLIVE OIL
2 TABLESPOONS DIJON MUSTARD
3 EGG WHITES

CHIPS
3 POUNDS RUSSET POTATOES

Pad thai is full of wonderfully complementary ingredients, such as the mild earthy flavors of peanuts and rice noodles, the sweet of tamarind and lime juice, and a little heat. The malty and well-hopped character of the Hugh Malone makes for a great eating companion, especially if you make the pad thai on the spicy side. Hugh's pleasantly dry finish balances each sweet, sour, and spiced bite and prepares you for the next one.

# PAD THAI

Begin with soaking the noodles in lukewarm water—careful not to let them get too soft.

In a large skillet (or wok), over high heat, add the grapeseed oil and sauté the shallot, garlic, and tofu until golden brown. Add the tamarind paste, cane sugar, fish sauce, chili pepper, and black pepper and cook for 1 to 2 minutes.

Drain the noodles, add them to the skillet, and cook until just heated through (about 30 seconds). Crack the egg into the noodles and stir, cooking for about 1 minute.

In a small bowl of ice water, add the lemon juice and soak the banana flower for 15 minutes. Strain and then stir in with the noodles. Add bean sprouts, peanuts, chives, and lime juice and serve immediately.

8 OUNCES THAI RICE NOODLES (½ PACKAGE)
2 TABLESPOONS GRAPESEED OIL
1 SHALLOT, MINCED
3 CLOVES GARLIC, MINCED
¼ CUP EXTRA FIRM TOFU, CUBED OR CRUMBLED
2 TABLESPOONS TAMARIND PASTE
2 TABLESPOONS CANE SUGAR
4 TEASPOONS THAI FISH SAUCE
½ TEASPOON GROUND CHILI PEPPER
FRESHLY GROUND PEPPER

1 LARGE EGG
½ POUND SHRIMP, STEAMED
1⅓ CUPS BEAN SPROUTS
¾ CUP GROUND PEANUTS
½ CUP CHOPPED CHIVES
JUICE FROM ONE LIME

½ BANANA FLOWER BUD, STEAMED
JUICE FROM ONE LEMON

There was a moment when I felt as if this dish might need a vegetable with it, but it passed. Pair this great cut of (hopefully local) meat with a simple and flavor-packed cream sauce of black pepper and rosemary. The rich savory canvas of steak and cream serves to heighten both the spices in the sauce and the excellent aromatic qualities of the Hugh Malone ale.

## New York Strip Steak with IPA Cream Sauce

Preheat oven to 200°F or warm.

Allow steak to come to room temperature and season with salt and pepper.

In a skillet, over high heat, cook steaks until desired temperature is reached (3 to 4 minutes a side for medium-rare to medium). Remove the steak from the pan and allow to rest in the warm oven while making the sauce.

### SAUCE
In the same skillet used to cook the steaks, add the beef broth to deglaze the pan. Scrape the bottom of the pan to release the bits from the steak. Reduce the broth by about half, then add the Hugh Malone, heavy cream, butter, black pepper, and rosemary.

Reduce the mixture until it thickens slightly.

Plate the steaks, cover with cream sauce, and serve immediately.

4 NEW YORK STRIP STEAKS
  (APPROXIMATELY 1 INCH THICK AND 8 OUNCES)
SALT AND PEPPER, TO TASTE

SAUCE
3 OUNCES BEEF BROTH
3 OUNCES HUGH MALONE ALE
¾ CUP HEAVY CREAM
2 TABLESPOONS CLARIFIED BUTTER
¼ TEASPOON BLACK PEPPERCORNS,
  COARSELY GROUND
½ TEASPOON FRESH ROSEMARY, FINELY
  CHOPPED

Extremely popular down South, especially in Louisiana, everyone's gumbo (or their mother's) is the best of course—but this recipe might be your close second. The wonderful dark spice of andouille sausage and browned roux make for a great contrast to the brighter, bittersweet profile of the Hugh Malone. Easily one of the tasting team's favorite combinations!

# GUMBO

In a Dutch oven or cocotte, brown the sausage in the olive oil, remove, and set aside. Do the same with the chicken.

Combine the flour and butter to form a roux, then add to the cocotte and cook over medium heat until brown, stirring constantly.

Add the onion, garlic, green pepper, and fennel and mix well. Cook for 5 to 6 minutes or until the vegetables soften. Add the beef broth, Worcestershire sauce, one-quarter of the chopped parsley, cayenne pepper, and salt and pepper and then bring to a boil.

Reduce the heat and add the chicken and sausage and simmer for approximately 30 minutes. Add the tomatoes and okra and simmer for another hour or so. Turn off the heat, add shrimp, and cover, letting them cook over the next 15 minutes.

Just before serving, check seasoning, then add the scallions and chopped parsley.

Serve over rice.

¼ CUP OLIVE OIL
1 POUND ANDOUILLE SAUSAGE, SLICED THIN (¼-INCH)
6 CHICKEN THIGHS (SKINLESS), CUT IN BITE-SIZED PIECES
2½ OUNCES FLOUR
2½ OUNCES BUTTER
1 YELLOW ONION, MEDIUM DICE
8 CLOVES GARLIC, MINCED
1 GREEN PEPPER, SEEDED AND CHOPPED
1 FENNEL BULB, MEDIUM DICE
4 CUPS BEEF BROTH
¼ CUP WORCESTERSHIRE SAUCE
PINCH CAYENNE PEPPER
SALT AND PEPPER, TO TASTE
1 CAN WHOLE TOMATOES (14-OUNCE), ROUGH CHOP
2 OUNCES OKRA, SLICED THIN
8 OUNCES SHRIMP (26/30)
4 SCALLIONS, SLICED THIN
¼ BUNCH FLAT-LEAF PARSLEY, CHOPPED COARSE, PLUS A FEW LEAVES FOR GARNISH

## CHEF'S NOTES

Roux is usually used along a color scale with markers being blonde, brown, or dark depending on how long the flour is toasted and the desired flavor. Here, a dark brown roux gives plenty of flavor as well as providing gumbo's traditional color.

Gumbo, like most soups and stews, benefits from time. If possible, make it a day ahead of schedule to let the flavors come together. It takes a little patience and restraint, but it's worth it.

I really liked the savory-sweet of salted caramel alongside the crisp and delightfully well-balanced hop flavor of the Hugh Malone. In its American-Belgian style, Allagash provides a wonderful example of a traditional hop-heavy IPA, while weaving the usual bitterness in and out of the fruity, dulcet tones of Belgian yeast.

# OLD SALT CARAMELS

Using an 8-inch-square baking dish (or smaller for thicker candies), completely line with parchment paper and then coat the parchment with nonstick cooking spray.

In a saucepan, bring the cream, butter, and salt to a boil. Remove from heat and set aside.

In a larger saucepan, combine the sugar, corn syrup, and water and bring to a boil, stirring occasionally until the sugar dissolves. Caramelize the sugar to the color you wish to achieve (sweeter or richer), gently moving the pan to keep the color consistent throughout.

Carefully, add the cream mixture to the caramel (it will bubble up), and stir to incorporate.

Using a candy or deep-fry thermometer, cook the caramel mixture to the "firm-ball" stage, between 245° to 250°F, then pour immediately into the lined baking dish.

Let cool for several hours, then sprinkle on additional fleur de sel for decoration and a salty crunch.

Cut into 1-inch pieces and serve; or wrap each piece in squares of wax paper big enough to twist closed (3 to 4 inches).

1 CUP HEAVY CREAM
2½ OUNCES (5 TABLESPOONS) UNSALTED
 BUTTER, CUT INTO SMALL CUBES
1 TEASPOON FLEUR DE SEL
 (OR ½ TEASPOON FINE SEA SALT)
1½ CUPS SUGAR
¼ CUP LIGHT CORN SYRUP
¼ CUP WATER

$C_{21}H_{30}O_5$

2011

# HUGH MALONE
## ALE

ALLAGASH

# Hugh Malone

Hugh Malone begins with a grain bill featuring a blend of Maine-grown barley, imported pilsner, and raw wheat malt. At the beginning of run off, we add a portion of hops to the sweet wort in the kettle, a technique known as "first wort hopping." As the boil begins, a generous amount of Chinook hops are added for bittering. Later, in the whirlpool, the beer is hopped with a blend of Centennial and Amarillo, for aroma. This same blend is used post fermentation, a process called dry hopping, to lend additional hop character to the finished beer. The result is a complex brew with a malty palate, intense hop aromas, pronounced bitterness, and a pleasantly dry finish.

Description: Belgian-Style IPA
ABV: 7.8%
Profile: Floral Nose, Fruity, Dry Finish
Serving Temperature: 40° to 50°F
Availability: Limited Annual Release
Package: 750ml bottle, 5.17 gallon keg
Ideal Within: Six Months

CHAPTER 10

# COOLSHIP

As the slogan "Always An Adventure" suggests, there is always something new in the works for fans of Allagash beer, whether tasting the Allagash versions of classic Belgian beers like the Tripel or a completely different style of beer like the Coolship series.

In the fall of 2007, Allagash built what's referred to as a coolship pan for inoculating its beers with naturally occurring wild yeast in the air around the brewery. The coolship is a large but shallow vat, allowing maximum exposure to air during the night, as well as permitting the brewed wort to cool more quickly. The cooled wort is then transferred into oak barrels where fermentation takes place, a process that can take up to three years to complete. It's not ready until it is deemed ready by the brewing team.

Allagash makes several individual types of Coolship beer. The Resurgam is a blend of one-, two-, and three-year-old, unfruited coolship beer, while both the Cerise and Balaton are made by adding select cherry varieties to the coolship beer at the end of the aging process. Coolship Red is aged with raspberries. As delicious as these beers sound (and are), don't hold your breath for a big release into the marketplace. The batches are made available gradually, in very small amounts, and without much promotion. Allagash keeps the program low-profile so more visitors to the brewery will have a chance to sample them. Beer lovers would do well to plan their own sojourn to Portland, Maine, well in advance to increase the chances of walking away with a bottle or two.

Around the kitchen, the flavor profile of spontaneous beers provides a unique opportunity to play with your food—in the most grown-up way possible, of course. The recipes in this chapter, designed around the Coolship Cerise, are neither overly sweet nor distinctly savory, mimicking the flavor profile of the Cerise. Skeptics will be seduced by the absence of any syrupy quality and the wood-scented, antiqued cherry background, while the gourmand will find the drying finish an exquisite segue into the next bite, inviting future culinary experimentation for both. Anything else would be un-Allagash.

Peppadew peppers give this recipe its unique flavor and gentle spice. Their one-of-a-kind tang, along with the gentle brine of the shrimp, blends with the mellow, wood-tinged Balaton and Montmorency cherries used in the making of the Coolship Cerise. The result is a pairing that's unexpected and original—par for the course in Portland, Maine.

# SWEET AND SPICY SHRIMP

**GREEN BEANS**

Set a steamer basket insert into a saucepan and fill with water to just below the level of the steamer. Bring the water to a boil, add the green beans, and steam for approximately 6 minutes, or until they are tender to your liking. Season with salt and pepper.

**SHRIMP**

In a skillet, over medium-high heat, add the grapeseed oil and sauté the onion and garlic for 1 minute, then add the peppers and sauté another minute.

Add the shrimp and cook for about 2 minutes per side, then add the peppadew liquid and bring to a boil. Let boil for about 1 minute to finish cooking the shrimp.

Turn off the heat, add the chopped thyme and parsley, and mix well.

Serve with or over green beans.

**GREEN BEANS**
8 OUNCES FRESH GREEN BEANS, STEAMED
SALT AND PEPPER, TO TASTE

**SHRIMP**
1 TABLESPOON GRAPESEED OIL
¼ CUP YELLOW ONION, SMALL DICE
1 TEASPOON MINCED GARLIC
½ CUP PEPPADEW PEPPERS, THINLY SLICED
  AND ¼ CUP OF LIQUID RESERVED
12 OUNCES SHRIMP (26/30), PEELED AND
  DEVEINED, OR ABOUT 20 SHRIMP
½ TEASPOON FRESH THYME, FINELY
  CHOPPED
1 TABLESPOON CHOPPED FRESH PARSLEY

A client once described duck as "the red meat of birds," and while I think that may be a slight exaggeration, there's little doubt that roast duck carries loads of flavor. In this example, the whole bird is slow-roasted to bring out extra flavors and provide a smooth, moist texture. The blackberry gastrique (equal parts acid and sweetness) helps transition flavors from the duck to the Coolship Cerise— whose dry cherry and yeast character allows both sweet and savory pairings. This one is a little of both.

# SLOW-ROAST DUCK WITH BLACKBERRY GASTRIQUE

## DUCK
Preheat oven to 175°F.

Let duck come to room temperature and sprinkle with the 1 tablespoon of salt. Roast the duck until the internal temperature at the thigh joint is at least 150°F; depending on your duck this may take up to 6 hours (it's worth it). Remove the duck from the oven, cover, and let rest for 20 minutes.

In a saucepan, bring the water to a boil and then add the rice and butter. Simmer for 20 minutes, then turn off heat and let stand covered for 10 to 15 additional minutes. Uncover and strain.

Melt the butter over medium-high heat, then sauté the onions for 2 to 3 minutes or until they are soft. Stir in the pecans and dump the mixture in the rice, adding the sliced sage leaves. Mix thoroughly and check seasoning before serving with the duck. (If the duck is not ready, simply cover and keep warm until ready to serve.)

## BLACKBERRY GASTRIQUE
In a saucepan, bring the wine and vinegar to a boil. Reduce heat slightly and reduce volume by half. When the wine-vinegar mixture is reduced, add the blackberries and set aside.

**DUCK**
1 WHOLE DUCK (5 TO 6 POUNDS)
1 TABLESPOON + 1 TEASPOON SALT, SEPARATED

2 CUPS BROWN RICE
3 CUPS WATER
1 TABLESPOON BUTTER
PINCH OF SALT

4 TABLESPOONS UNSALTED BUTTER
1 YELLOW ONION, SMALL DICE
¾ CUP CHOPPED PECANS
3 TO 4 SAGE LEAVES, ROLLED AND THINLY SLICED

**BLACKBERRY GASTRIQUE**
4 CUPS DRY RED WINE
1 CUP BANYULS (OR SHERRY) VINEGAR
4 CUPS FRESH BLACKBERRIES
2 CUPS SUGAR
2 OUNCES WATER, PLUS OR MINUS
JUICE OF 1 LEMON
⅛ TEASPOON CINNAMON

In another saucepan, make a paste from the sugar and water, then add ½ teaspoon of the lemon juice. Bring sugar mixture to a boil, reduce heat slightly, and let cook until the mixture begins to caramelize (turn brown) around the edges of the pan, stirring occasionally to make the color uniform.

Let the sugar cook until a light amber color is achieved throughout. While stirring, carefully pour in the wine mixture and blackberries. You may reduce the sauce further if you would like a thicker texture—you can also purée the sauce if you wish. To the final sauce, add the cinnamon and brighten the mixture to taste with the remaining lemon juice.

A deceptively simple dish to make for the enjoyment it can produce, the salsa is best made a couple of hours ahead of the meal to let flavors combine and blend. The swordfish is brought to life by grilling, and the sweet heat of the salsa fresca works as a great complement to the dry, antique cherry fruit of the Coolship. Make this one several times during tomato season.

# GRILLED SWORDFISH WITH PEACH SALSA FRESCA

**PEACH SALSA FRESCA**

In a mixing bowl, add the peaches, tomato, and red onion and mix.

Combine the rest of the ingredients with the peach mixture and gently mix until uniform.

Check seasoning, cover, and set aside.

**SWORDFISH**

Preheat grill or grill pan and prep with nonstick spray or wipe on grapeseed oil with a cloth.

Rub each side of the swordfish with a bit of oil and season with salt and pepper. When the grill or pan is ready, cook the fish for about 4 minutes on each side, turning 45 to 90 degrees after a couple of minutes to create grill marks, if you wish.

Since swordfish steaks can vary greatly in thickness, use a meat thermometer to prevent drying out, ensuring that the internal temperature doesn't go beyond 125°F.

**PEACH SALSA FRESCA**
2 CUPS FRESH PEACHES, SMALL DICE
1 ROMA TOMATO, SMALL DICE
½ CUP RED ONION, SMALL DICE
1 JALAPEÑO PEPPER, SEEDED AND FINELY
 DICED
JUICE FROM 1 LIME
2 DASHES TABASCO SAUCE
1 TABLESPOON FINELY CHOPPED
 CILANTRO
SALT AND PEPPER, TO TASTE

**SWORDFISH**
2 POUNDS SWORDFISH (ENOUGH FOR 4
 TO 6 PEOPLE)
GRAPESEED OIL
SEA SALT
FRESHLY GROUND PEPPER

A few components from the Mexican molé sauce are more simply combined, but you won't miss out on the rich flavors of chocolate, dried chiles, and peanuts. The Coolship Cerise's brassy cherry flavor is enhanced by the dark savory of the chicken, and the beer's elegant and drying finish helps refresh the palate. A unique and highly suitable duo.

## CHICKEN, CHOCOLATE, AND CHILES

Wearing latex gloves, remove the stem and seeds from the chiles.

In a large skillet, over medium heat, heat about half the butter, then add the chiles, onion, and garlic and cook for 3 to 4 minutes, or just softened. Transfer the mixture to a soup pot.

Add the remaining butter to the skillet and cook the plantain pieces until browned, about 3 to 4 minutes. Remove plantains, place on a paper towel, and let cool. Chop tortillas into medium-size pieces and cook briefly in the pan on each side.

In a double boiler, heat the peanut butter, honey, sesame seeds, chili powder, cumin, cloves, cinnamon, and chocolate, stirring every so often and until the mixture is uniform. Add the peanut butter mixture to the soup pot. Add the diced tomatoes and chicken broth to the soup pot and let simmer and develop for 20 to 30 minutes. Purée the mixture in a blender until smooth and then pass through a fine-mesh strainer. Check seasoning, cover, and set aside to mature.

Place the chicken into an ovenproof ceramic Dutch oven. Cover the chicken with the chile-chocolate sauce and simmer over medium-low heat until the chicken is cooked through. You can also cook the chicken separately and then cover with the chile-chocolate sauce.

Garnish with fried plantains and tortillas.

3 PLUS TABLESPOONS BUTTER
10 DRIED CHILES (CHIPOTLE, ANCHO, OR GUAJILLO)
1 LARGE ONION, MEDIUM DICE
4 CLOVES GARLIC, MINCED

1 PLANTAIN, MEDIUM DICE
4 TO 6 CORN TORTILLAS, THINLY SLICED

½ CUP UNSWEETENED PEANUT BUTTER
¼ CUP HONEY
2 TABLESPOONS SESAME SEEDS
1 TABLESPOON CHILI POWDER (SPICY, IF YOU LIKE)
1 TEASPOON GROUND CUMIN
⅛ TEASPOON GROUND CLOVES
½ TEASPOON GROUND CINNAMON
2 OUNCES DARK CHOCOLATE CHIPS/ SMALL PIECES
ONE 14-OUNCE CAN DICED TOMATOES, APPROXIMATELY 6 SMALL FRESH TOMATOES
2 PLUS CUPS CHICKEN BROTH (OR STOCK)
3 POUNDS CHICKEN
SALT AND PEPPER, TO TASTE

Before drinking my first bottle of Coolship, I wondered if a cherry pie might be good with it, but then I thought it might be too obvious of a pairing. The vanilla bean and brown sugar help enrich the flavor of the cherries and provide a warm, semisweet companion to the tart, dry fruit notes in the Cerise.

# A Simple Cherry Pie

**PIE DOUGH**

Put the flour, salt, and sugar in the mixing bowl of a countertop mixer fitted with the paddle attachment. Add the butter to the flour mixture and turn the mixer on the lowest possible speed. Watch the mix carefully as the mixer works the butter into the flour, turning off the mixer here and there to check the size of the remaining butter. Stop mixing when any remaining pieces of butter are about the size of peas. Strain any ice cubes out from the water and turn the mixer back on low speed, carefully adding the ice water a tablespoon at a time and letting each addition mix in for a few seconds before adding more. The dough is done when a small addition of water begins to peel the dough back cleanly from the edges of the mixing bowl (probably well before you add the entire 4 ounces). Divide into two balls, flatten them into small disks, and refrigerate for about an hour.

**PIE FILLING**

Place the cherries in a large mixing bowl. Combine several ounces of the cold water with the cornstarch to make a slurry. In a saucepan, over medium-high heat, add the remaining water, the slurry, cherry juice, salt, cinnamon, and vanilla scrapings; the mixture will start to thicken. Turn the heat down and cook the mixture for about a minute, then pour over the cherries and fold until uniform. Set aside and let cool while you roll the pie dough.

**TO ASSEMBLE**

Preheat oven to 350°F.

**PIE DOUGH**
(ENOUGH FOR A 9-INCH PIE WITH A
  LATTICE OR FULL TOP)
12 OUNCES FLOUR (A LITTLE MORE THAN
  2 CUPS)
½ TEASPOON SALT
1 TEASPOON SUGAR
8 OUNCES (2 STICKS) COLD BUTTER, CUT
  IN SMALL CUBES
½ CUP ICE WATER (YOU WON'T USE IT ALL)

**PIE FILLING**
1 CUP COLD WATER
1 CUP CHERRY JUICE
¼ CUP CORNSTARCH
1 (SCANT) CUP LIGHT BROWN SUGAR
¼ TEASPOON SALT
⅛ TEASPOON GROUND CINNAMON
1 VANILLA BEAN, SEEDS SCRAPED AND
  RESERVED
2 TO 2½ POUNDS CHERRIES, PITTED

In a mixing bowl, add the egg and water and whisk to incorporate; place a pastry brush nearby and set all aside. Roll out first dough disk to about ⅛-inch thickness and cut an 11- to 12-inch circle, then set aside. Center the dough on a pie pan, ensuring that it molds well to the shape of the pan. Put the cherry mixture in the pie crust and spread evenly. Roll out the second dough disk in the same manner, making the same 11- to 12-inch circle. Coat the bottom dough's exposed edge in the egg wash and add the top circle to the pie, crimping the edges to combine and removing any visible flour with the pastry brush. Coat the entire top of the pie with the egg mixture, vent the pie with several well-placed slits in the top, and place in the oven. Cook for about an hour, or until the filling can be seen cooked near the top vent slits. Let cool completely before serving.

# COOLSHIP

Coolship Cerise is brewed using a large portion of unmalted wheat, which is very traditional to the brewing of spontaneously fermented beers. The mash is also heated up throughout the brewing, a process known as step mashing. This creates better enzyme conversion and produces the types of sugar desired in the long-term fermentation of a spontaneous beer. The yeast for fermentation is derived 100% from the air, as the wort is cooled overnight in the coolship. Unlike traditionally produced beers, which ferment in stainless tanks, Coolship fermentation takes place inside of oak barrels. This process can take 3 to 4 years. The results of this lengthy fermentation are complex flavors like unripe fruit, leather, citrus, and oak and a dry, tart finish. The Coolship Cerise has the addition of cherries for the last six months of aging, which adds another layer of complexity and color. The sweet and tart character of the cherries plays off the dry and tart profile of the base beer. Using only local Maine cherries, and yeast from the Portland air to ferment, the Coolship Cerise is a true reflection of Allagash terrior.

Description: Belgian Strong Ale Brewed with White Grapes
ABV: 9%
Profile: Golden, Fresh Cucumber, Vinous, Slight Pepper
Serving Temperature: 40° to 50°F
Availability: Limited Annual Release
Package: 750ml bottle, 5.17 gallon keg
Ideal Within: Two Years

# ACKNOWLEDGMENTS

To my aunt, Gerri Strigle, the first person to believe that cooking was my future—and hire me. Best. Martini. Party. Ever.

Much appreciation to Dee Dee and Rob at Allagash for not thinking I was making prank calls when I first contacted them.

My cocreator, Brian Smestad, well, isn't this great? I really appreciate these last two years and all that's still to come. How'd this happen, again? Oh, right . . . beer.

Many thanks to Dave P. for letting us use the hacienda for a couple of weeks. We came early, stayed late, and invited people you didn't know—and you welcomed it!

Love to Jeff, Kimberly, and Angie at Blue Tree and The Branch Creative—you guys turn hard work into play! Let's do it again.

To Carmen Janette . . . because we're the same person. To Joyce P., I did the work, and the cherry pie is for you. Thanks to Stan Riley at Holy Smoke BBQ in Columbus, Ohio, for his advice and counsel on smoking just about anything.

For my parents, who have learned to love and support me through anything. And actually like it.

—James Simpkins


My thanks to James for sharing his genuine passion for food and with it, the journey we have traveled on this project.

Deep appreciation is due Rob, Dee Dee, and the entire Allagash team for their enthusiasm over the last two years.

Sincere thanks to my good friend Dave Pelletier, for listening and embracing my vision from the outset. And a debt of gratitude to my friends and family and everyone I work with—their support has made this dream happen.

—Brian Smestad

# GLOSSARY

**ABV**

Alcohol by Volume. The measure of the amount of space the alcohol in beer takes up as a percentage of total volume.

**ALE**

Beers made with a strain of yeast that ferments at the top of a fermentation tank. Ales typically have a more pronounced yeast presence.

**ALLAGASH**

The Allagash Wilderness Waterway is an area in rural northern Maine that is part of the National Wild and Scenic River System. The word *Allagash* comes from the Penobscot Indian word meaning "bark stream."

**BOTTLE CONDITIONING**

A secondary fermentation that takes place when yeast and sugar are added to a beer right before bottling. This process is used to carbonate a beer, instead of forcing $CO_2$ into it. Bottle conditioning adds more complexity and a longer shelf life.

**BRETTANOMYCES**

A type of yeast that lives on the skin of fruits. Traditionally considered a beer spoiler, it has most recently become a more accepted yeast in the production of beers, especially traditional Belgian styles.

## CANDI SUGAR

A non-malt fermentable that can be added to beer to raise the alcohol, make the beer drier, and/or to add certain flavors. Candi sugars vary in color from light to dark. Most candi sugar is derived from beet sugar.

## COOLSHIP

A large shallow vessel used for cooling hot wort while leaving it exposed to yeasts that are in the air.

## FERMENTATION

The process in which yeast consumes sugars to produce alcohol and CO2.

## HIGH GRAVITY

In reference to the total amount of sugar available for fermentation in the wort produced for beer. High gravity is another way to reference high alcohol in a beer.

## HOPS

The blossom of a climbing herb known as *Humulus Lupulus*. Hops are responsible for bitterness in beer.

## LAGER

A beer produced by using a bottom-fermenting yeast strain. Typically low in alcohol, light in color, and clean in flavor.

## MALT

Barley that has been steeped in water, allowed to germinate, and then dried to stop germination. A primary ingredient in beer, malt is a source of fermentable sugars, flavor, and body.

## MASH

The slurry created when combining malt with water in order to extract the fermentable sugars.

## SPONTANEOUS FERMENTATION

The process of fermentation in which the yeast is not mechanically added but rather allowed to inoculate the wort by leaving the wort exposed to the open air where yeast is constantly present.

## STEP MASHING

A mash schedule that features upward steps in rest temperatures to allow for optimum enzyme conversion.

## TRAPPIST

A member of the main branch of the Cistercian monks. There are currently seven Trappist monasteries, six in Belgium and one in the Netherlands, that produce beer.

## WORT

The sugary liquid produced by combining malt and water.

## YEAST

Single-celled organisms responsible for converting the sugars produced in brewing into alcohol and $CO_2$.

# INDEX

## A

Aioli, 49
 White Aioli, 21
Allspcice, 91
Almond Flour, 55
Almonds, Sliced, 55
Ancho Chili Powder, 123
Apple, 85, 91, 93
Apricot Preserves, 79
Arugula, 53, 83, 93
Avocado, 121

## B

Bacon, 35, 63, 67, 95, 97, 107
Banana Flower Bud, 135
Barley, 63
Beans
 Black, 37
 Green, 27, 147
 White, 107
Beef
 Burger, 109
 Chuck, 124
 Cottage Pie, 105
 Meatloaf, 97
 New York Strip Steak, 137
 Pot Roast, 124

 Stew, 63
Bibb lettuce, 55
Blackberry Gastrique, 149
Bourbon Butter, 77
Brandy, 127
Bread, Sourdough, 39
Brown Rice, 149
Buttermilk, 85
Butternut Squash, 65, 119

## C

Cabbage, 121
Capers, 69
Caponata, 69
Cardamom, 85
Carrots, 23, 105, 121
Cayenne Pepper, 21
Celery, 49, 69
Celery Seed, 23, 121
Cheese
 Blue, 111
 Cheddar, Burger, 109
 Cheddar Grilled Cheese, 83
 Cheddar Salad, 93
 Farmer's, 37, 105
 Feta, 81
 Gorgonzola, 65
 Mozzarella, 97

Parmesan, 65, 81, 97, 107

Stilton, 53

Cherries, Pitted 155, Juice 155

Chiles

Ancho, 153

Chipotle, 109, 153

Guajillo, 153

Molé, 153

Chili, 111

Chili Powder, 37, 111, 153

Chives, 135

Chocolate

Bittersweet Chocolate Chips, 113

Chocolate, Dark, 67

Chocolate Malt Powder, 67

Cocoa Powder, Unsweetened, 43

Dark Chocolate Chips, 153

Cilantro, 51, 111, 151

Cloves, 91, 153

Coconut, 51

Coffee, 111

Collard Greens, 35

Corn, 37

Corn Syrup, 141

Cornmeal, 29, 119

Crab, 21, 55

Cranberries, 53, 91

Crème Fraîche, 39, 63

Custard, 71

## D

Dressing, Salad, 49, 53

Dry Rub Spice, 123

Dough

Pie, 155

Pizza, 81

Puff Pastry, 98

## E

Eggplants, 69

Escarole, 23

## F

Fennel Bulb, 23, 63, 69, 125, 139

Fennel Seeds, 125

Fleur De Sel, 141

Frisée Lettuce, 53

## G

Game

Buffalo, 111

Duck, 149

Venison, 91

Garlic Powder, 123

Garnish, 39, 111

Gelatin, 57

Ginger Root, 85

Ginger, Ground, 43, 79, 91, 127

Gougeres, 111

Gumbo, 139

## H

Hominy, 25

Honey, 29, 53, 79

Hot Sauce, 51, 111, 121

## J

Jalapeño Pepper, 79, 151

## K

Kale, 23, 95

## L

Lamb, 41, 69, 107

Licorice, Black, 71

Lime, 37, 79, 121, 135
Lobster, 49

**M**

Mango, 49, 55, 79
Marinade, 121
Mayonnaise, 121
Mint, 107
Mushrooms, 37

**N**

Nutmeg, 65, 85, 113

**O**

Okra, 139
Olives, 69, 125
Onion
  Powder, 123
  Scallion, 49, 93, 121, 139
  Sweet, 79

**P**

Panko Bread Crumbs, 97
Paprika, 79, 111, 119
Paprika, Smoked, 111
Parsley, Flat-leaf, 23
Parsnips, 63, 125
Passion Fruit, 57
Pastry Cream, Rosemary, 98
Peanuts, 135
Pear, 53
Pecans, 93, 149
Peppers
  Peppadew, 147
  Red Bell, 37, 93
Pesto, 107
Pine Nuts, 51, 69, 107

Pizza, 81
Plantain, 51, 153
Plums, Dried, 127
Poppy Seeds, 79
Pork
  Prosciutto, 51
  Ribs, 123
  Shoulder, 25
  Tenderloin, 95
Potatoes
  Red, 27
  Russet, 63, 105, 133
Poultry
*Chicken*
  Breast, 51, 93, 153
  Roulades, 51
  Sausage, 81
  Thighs, 139
  Whole, 35
*Duck*, 149

**Q**

Quinoa, 37

**R**

Raisins, Glolden, 69, 85
Red Pepper Flakes, 85, 111
Relish, 91
Rice Noodles, 135
Romaine Leaves, 93

**S**

Salads
  Cheddar Salad, 93
  Pear Salad, 53
  Spinach Salad, 79
Sauces and Chutneys

Aioli, 49
Blackberry Gastrique, 149
Caribbean BBQ, 79
Chutney, Apple, 85
Cilantro-Mint, 51
IPA Cream Sauce, 137
Peach Salsa Fresca, 151
Simple Sauce (Lamb), 41
Simple Sauce (Meatloaf), 97
Simple Sauce (Pot Roast), 125
Sweet Mustard, 95
White Aioli, 21
Seafood and Shellfish
  Cod, 27, 133
  Grouper, 79
  Oysters, 119
  Scallops, 77
  Shrimp, 135, 139, 147
  Snapper, 121
  Swordfish, 151
Shallots, 107, 135
Shortbread, 71
Spinach, 65, 79, 81, 97
Sugar
  Brown, 85, 95, 127, 155
  Cane, 135
  Confectioners, 71
Sweet Potato, 39

## T
Tabasco, 151
Tarragon, 45
Tart, 65
Thyme, 21, 23
Tofu, 135
Tomatoes
  Heirloom, 27
  Purée, 69
  Roma, 151
  Sun-Dried, 81
Tortillas, 121, 153

## V
Vanilla Bean, 57, 85, 99, 155
Vanilla Extract, 71, 113
Vinegar
  Apple Cider, 25, 35
  Balsamic, 53, 95
  Red Wine, 69
  Rice Wine, 51
  White Wine, 79

## W
Waffles, 85
Walnuts, 39, 53
Water Chestnuts, 67
White Pepper, Ground, 51
Worcestershire Sauce, 95, 97, 139

Wine
  Red Wine, 41, 111, 125, 149
  White Wine, 39, 55, 69, 95

## Z
Zucchini, 37